Optimum Currency Areas
New Analytical and Policy Developments

Editors
**Mario I. Blejer, Jacob A. Frenkel,
Leonardo Leiderman, and Assaf Razin,
in cooperation with David M. Cheney**

International Monetary Fund
1997

Cover design by Massoud Etemadi and interior design by Julio Prego
IMF Graphics Section

Library of Congress Cataloging-in-Publication Data

Optimum currency areas: new analytical and policy developments /
   editors, Mario I. Blejer, Jacob A. Frenkel, Leonardo Leiderman, and
   Assaf Razin; in cooperation with David M. Cheney.
      p. cm.
         Includes bibliographical references (p.).
         ISBN 1–55775–652-X (pbk.)

   1. Monetary unions.   2. Monetary policy.   I. Frenkel, Jacob A.
II. Leiderman, Leonardo, 1951- .   III. Razin, Assaf.   IV. Cheney, David M.
V. Title.
HG3894.B58 1997
332.4'6—dc21   97–13514
                                                                                    CIP

Price: US$15.00

recycled paper

Address orders to:
International Monetary Fund, Publication Services
700 19th Street, N.W., Washington, D.C. 20431, U.S.A.
Telephone: (202) 623–7430
Telefax: (202) 623–7201
E-mail: publications@imf.org
Internet: http://www.imf.org

CONTENTS

Preface

THE ONGOING PROCESS OF ECONOMIC INTEGRATION IN EUROPE—with monetary integration and the creation of a single European currency critical elements of the process—has renewed interest in the concept of an optimum currency area. In recent years, many economists have written in search of an appropriate analytical framework to permit the evaluation of the requirements for, and consequences of, monetary integration. And, as is often the case, they begin with the concept of an optimum currency area pioneered by Robert A. Mundell in 1961.

This volume is the result of a December 1996 symposium on optimum currency areas, held in Tel Aviv and sponsored by the Bank of Israel, the IMF, and Tel Aviv and Hebrew Universities. The symposium, and this book, honor Robert Mundell and his seminal contribution to this and many other important topics. They do that in part by providing an opportunity for him to reflect on and update his thinking on the subject, and by asking other distinguished experts to present their views on the theoretical and policy-oriented implications of Mundell's original contribution—and its relevance for European economic and monetary union (EMU).

The run-up to the launching of EMU on January 1, 1999, is indeed a heady period, given the scope and magnitude of the project. The IMF recently hosted a conference on EMU and its implications for the IMF and for the international monetary system, which considered the issues of timing, the euro's strength as a currency, the impact on the stability of exchange rates, and how the IMF should adapt.

This timely book sheds light on many of the relevant issues. It offers thoughts and concepts that extend and clarify the analytical framework for assessing the implications and consequences of EMU, which is clearly the most important outstanding issue for the international monetary system.

It is entirely appropriate for the IMF to salute, on his sixty-fifth birthday, Bob Mundell, whose work—some of it done at the IMF—guides so

1

many of us in our thinking about exchange rates and the international economy. To Bob we say, well done and thank you for all you have contributed.

Stanley Fischer
First Deputy Managing Director
International Monetary Fund

Acknowledgments

THE DISCUSSIONS HELD IN TEL AVIV during the December 4–6, 1996, conference, "Optimum Currency Areas: The Current Agenda for International Monetary and Fiscal Integration," commemorated the thirty-fifth anniversary of Robert Mundell's seminal article on optimum currency areas. They also sought to shed light on the relevance of OCA theory for the impending European economic and monetary union.

We would like to extend our appreciation to Robert Mundell for his updating of the agenda for monetary union provided in Tel Aviv and to all participants in the conference. We are especially grateful to the joint sponsors of the conference: the Bank of Israel, the International Monetary Fund, The Pinhas Sapir Center for Development and The Rubinstein Foundation at Tel Aviv University, and The Helmut Kohl Institute for European Studies at the Hebrew University of Jerusalem. Thanks are also owed to Nava Ganor, for her organizational support, and to Lijun Li for wordprocessing.

Mario I. Blejer
Jacob A. Frenkel
Leonardo Leiderman
Assaf Razin
David M. Cheney

1

Introduction

Introduction

Mario I. Blejer, Leonardo Leiderman, and Assaf Razin

Dealing with intellectual history and, in particular, contemporary intellectual history, is indeed a dangerous undertaking. Any attempt to ascertain the origin of ideas and pin them down to a definite source always seems to raise a scholarly challenge and to invite claims that the idea under discussion has already been the subject of consideration and deliberation. Evidently, however, not everything has been said before. And certain ideas can be traced, without too much effort and without generating too much controversy, to their precise intellectual source.

That is, indeed, the case of the theory of optimum currency areas, pioneered by Robert A. Mundell in the 1960s. In his classical article, published in 1961 in the *American Economic Review* and reprinted in this book, Mundell defined the notion and posed, for the first time, the optimum currency area (OCA) problem. His paper generated an immediate chain reaction, with later contributions extending, improving, qualifying, and building upon the concept. The practical implications of the theory, however, did not appear to have particularly immediate consequences, except perhaps in the context of the fixed-versus-flexible-exchange-rate debate. Therefore, interest in the subject appears to have faded over time.

The dynamics of the current process of economic integration in Europe have clearly reversed that trend. Developments in Europe have been such that, by the second half of the 1980s, the issue of monetary unification and the creation of a single European currency became the centerpiece of the integration process. It could be claimed (Eichengreen, 1993) that the momentous enterprise of creating a single currency in Europe is neither the exclusive product of analytical thinking, nor a necessary corollary of the materialization of the single market in capital, labor, and goods—but rather the consequence of political economy considerations. Even if this is so, it is still true that the debate over monetary unification in Europe has prompted an intense search for an appropriate analytical framework to allow an adequate evaluation of the requirements and consequences of the process. Invariably, the point of departure of this search has been Mundell's concept of an optimum currency area. This notion has, therefore, returned to center stage of economic policy debates, and as European economic and monetary union (EMU) draws nearer, it is important to focus again on the theoretical, analytical, and policy-oriented implications of Mundell's seminal contribution.

As Corden (1993) recently pointed out, re-reading Mundell is a rewarding experience. Despite the rapid transformations of world economic conditions, the central part of Mundell's analysis stands up well and continues to be highly relevant. The core of his thesis is that countries or regions constitute an optimum currency area when the real benefits for their economies of fixing irreversibly their exchange rates (or, in practice, adopting a single currency) exceed the real costs. This is, of course, the case when prices of goods and factors of production are perfectly flexible. But, as Mundell indicates, it is also the case when labor and capital are perfectly mobile among the countries or regions in question (Kenen, 1995). Although the essence of this insight remains unquestionable, the new wave of literature on monetary integration that flourished in the last decade has sought to adapt these original ideas to current world conditions (and, more specifically, to European conditions); it has also tried to provide new understandings of the factors that condition the existence of an optimum currency area, as well as the macroeconomic implications for an individual country of surrendering monetary and exchange rate policy instruments.

This new body of literature is too vast to be surveyed comprehensively. In this volume, we attempt to provide a brief primer on the subject. The book is divided into three sections. The first concentrates on Mundell's contributions—including a reprint of his original article and an update on the issue from a 1996 perspective. Mundell provides current views on the factors affecting a country's decision to join a currency union, and assesses the union's chances of success and the scope of EMU. The second section consists of a discussion—in the form of a policy forum—centering on the issue of the exchange rate regime. It evaluates, in the context of current world circumstances, the new analytical and policy-oriented developments regarding the classic fixed-versus-floating-exchange-rate debate. The third section constitutes a sampling of the new thoughts that have emerged around the subject of optimum currency areas as discussed in the December 1996 Tel Aviv symposium honoring Robert Mundell. These ideas are compiled in the form of short nontechnical papers (which are summaries of formal papers to be published elsewhere). They offer insights on the most pertinent considerations regarding the relevance of Mundell's contribution in the current context and demonstrate the continuing validity of his original concepts.

The papers reviewed in this book cover a variety of theoretical and empirical issues related to the theory of optimum currency areas and its current application to EMU. They can be grouped under four categories:

- a reassessment of the optimum currency area criteria and of the explicative power of the theory;
- a consideration of monetary policy issues within the EMU framework;
- fiscal and budgetary questions in the context of monetary unification; and
- the specific repercussions of the current drive toward EMU.

Reassessing OCA Criteria

While Mundell pointed out some of the theoretical considerations regarding the optimality of a single currency zone, some quantifiable parameters have been suggested as measures of the costs and benefits of joining a currency union. Two of the better-known among these parameters are the extent of trade and the correlation of shocks between countries contemplating monetary integration. In their paper, Jeffrey Frankel and Andrew Rose focus on an important observation: that trade patterns and income correlations are endogenous variables, in that they are not invariant to the degree of monetary integration among the countries considered. The econometric evidence they present is convincing: among most industrial countries, there is a positive relationship between the intensity of their bilateral trade and the nature of their business cycles. Thus, if monetary integration expands trade relations, it will also result in more correlated business cycles; countries are therefore more likely to satisfy the optimum currency area criteria ex post rather than ex ante.

Another of the well-known criteria postulated as determining the costs of monetary unification is economic openness. It has been widely claimed that the larger the degree of an economy's openness, the lower the cost of abandoning the nominal exchange rate as a policy instrument. Daniel Gros and Alfred Steinherr challenge the view that openness, per se, is a determining element. They conclude that one should look at the product of the degree of openness and of some measure of the importance of external shocks. A very open economy with an export structure very different from that of the other potential partners in a monetary union would lose much more from surrendering its ability to use the exchange rate than a much more closed economy with a similar export structure.

In addition to broad discussions dealing with the optimum currency area criteria, the literature has also addressed the predictive power of the theory. Tamim Bayoumi and Barry Eichengreen claim that optimum currency area theory has, indeed, significant explanatory power, particularly regarding the behavior of exchange rates. They find that variables pointed to by the theory affect the behavior of bilateral exchange rates through both market conditions and official intervention. Asymmetric shocks—one of the factors determining the cost of joining a monetary union—result in exchange rate variability, while the intensity of trade links (a source of benefits of a common currency) affect the exchange rate through the incentive to intervene. Therefore, the balance between these two factors, which are essential elements of the optimum currency area theory, could well explain the observed variability of exchange rates across countries.

Monetary Policy Issues in the EMU Framework

Beyond the question of suitable criteria for joining a monetary bloc, the major issues that have attracted interest in the recent debate relate to the operation of financial policies in the context of a single currency. Of those, of course, the implementation of uniform monetary policy across the members of a union, in place of national monetary policies, has received the greatest attention. In their paper, Thomas Krueger, Douglas Laxton, and Assaf Razin look at the alternative macroeconomic effects of alternative policy rules that could be adopted by the prospective European central bank at the inception of stage 3 of EMU—that is, the period following the irrevocable locking of exchange rates among the first group of countries qualified to participate. In assessing these effects, Krueger, Laxton, and Razin distinguish between the impact on EMU participants; on the group of countries that, in preparation for joining EMU later, will tie their currencies to the euro, through an ERM-type of exchange rate arrangement; and on those countries that would continue to follow their own monetary policies (Tabellini and Persson, 1966).

Through a number of simulation exercises, Krueger, Laxton, and Razin illustrate that an initial lack of credibility of the European central bank (particularly regarding anti-inflation policies) may introduce, in the short run, a deflationary bias for the EMU area. The effects are broadly the same for the second group of countries, namely, those that have tied their exchange rates to the euro. The deflationary effects, however, appear to be smaller for those countries that preserve their monetary independence. The authors conclude that such a bias should be considered by the European monetary authority since an attempt to build credibility too fast may be counterproductive if the costs, particularly in terms of unemployment, become politically intolerable.

The issue of limited credibility of monetary policies is also taken up in Alex Cukierman's paper, which focuses on the current Swedish situation. The paper examines the costs of weak credibility and assesses the relative advantages of different credibility-building institutions. Cukierman's main conclusion is that Sweden, one of the countries not expected to join EMU in the first round, should reform its monetary and fiscal institutions with a view to heightening the government commitment to price stability (and to embrace the Maastricht convergence criteria) in order to enhance its policy credibility and leave open the option of joining the monetary union later on.

Fiscal and Budgetary Issues

The theory of optimum currency areas does not advocate the abolition of independent budgetary responsibilities. In fact, the original formulations of the model have not been explicit about the specific roles of fiscal policy in the context of monetary unification. And, in practice, the conceptual framework within which EMU has evolved is one in which fiscal policies are indeed constrained, before and after joining the union, but, to a large extent, national budgetary operations remain much in the realm of individual country sovereignty.

The implications and potential conflicts associated with this setting are addressed in three papers in this book. The first paper, by Charles Goodhart, is strongly based on monetary doctrine. It claims that much of the debate on the boundaries for a single currency, and therefore, most of the discussions on the theory of optimum currency areas, has been based on the view that a currency's value depends primarily on the intrinsic value of that currency's backing. Goodhart advances the opposing view that a currency's value is based essentially on the power of the issuing authority, and therefore the extent of its use depends on considerations of political sovereignty. The key relationship arising from this alternative view is the strong link between political sovereignty and fiscal power, on the one hand, and money creation on the other. In this light, the EMU process appears unique: it is postulated upon divorcing the main monetary and fiscal authorities, which has not been seen before. Within this context, Goodhart claims, the market position of the domestic debt of the participating countries could weaken markedly. This, in his view, could lead to a shift in the focus of potential credibility crises and runs from the foreign exchange market toward sovereign bond markets.

Covering similar ground, but in a more policy-oriented framework, Roel Beetsma and Lans Bovenberg set up a formal model to analyze the consequences of monetary union with decentralized fiscal authorities. In contrast to the results suggested in the existing literature—which imply that such a setting produces pro-inflationary biases and excessive public spending—Beetsma and Bovenberg argue that monetary unification without coordination among autonomous fiscal powers may actually reduce the inflation bias and dampen any inclination toward increased public spending. They reason that a union containing noncooperative fiscal players strengthens the strategic position of the common central bank, which is always assumed to prefer lower inflation than the individual fiscal players. They claim further that the spending bias, and its inflationary consequences, falls as the number of countries within the union rises. Therefore, adding new participants to a monetary union raises the common welfare throughout the union. The argument of Beetsma and Bovenberg is also symmetrical: fiscal coordination among the members of a union strengthens the strategic position of the fiscal authorities against the common central bank and therefore leads to stronger inflationary propensities. The authors' argument supports, indeed, the subsidiarity principle regarding fiscal policy making.

Tamim Bayoumi and Paul Masson articulate an opposite view. Their reasoning focuses on the role and size of fiscal stabilizers, and they argue for conferring on a central union authority a significant role in fiscal stabilization. The argument of Bayoumi and Masson is based on Ricardian equivalence considerations. Indeed, if the private sector discounts the future tax liabilities arising from increased public debt and modifies its saving behavior accordingly, federal stabilizers will be more effective than local ones since local actions are more likely to be offset by the private sector. The same logic is used to claim that stabilization by national governments is likely to result in more offsetting behavior than an equivalent all-union policy. Based on their empirical results for Canada, the authors interpret their evidence as providing an argument for Europe to consider expanding fiscal policy at the union level.

Repercussions of the Move Toward EMU

As EMU draws nearer, some of its practical implications for both its members and the rest of the world are attracting greater attention. One of these issues, related to some extent to the previous discussion about the role of fiscal policies in a monetary union, is connected with the available mechanisms for achieving income insurance and consumption smoothing after the inception of EMU. Bent Sørensen and Oved Yosha study risk-sharing patterns among European Union members and OECD countries and compare them to their results for the United States.

The central finding of Sørenson and Yosha is that about 40 percent of the shocks to income are smoothed within a year, with roughly one-half the smoothing achieved through national government budget deficits. Their results also indicate that, unlike among individual states in the United States, factor income flows do not smooth income across countries in Europe, which suggests that European capital markets are less integrated than those in the United States. The main implication of these results is, in the authors' view, that the restrictions on budget deficits and public debt embodied in the Maastricht convergence criteria may threaten the stability of EMU in the absence of alternative risk-sharing mechanisms.

The last paper, by Fabio Ghironi and Francesco Giavazzi, deals with the size of EMU and the exchange rate regime that would emerge between the euro and the currencies of other EU countries. The authors suggest that the decision, in 1998, about the initial size of EMU will create substantial strain among the various players, with the outcome decided largely on the basis of the relative bargaining powers of the various policy makers. Once the initial size is decided, however, the propensity will be toward enlargement to cover the entire European Union, but the process could prove slower and more contentious than expected. Therefore, the question of the exchange rate regime between ins and outs is still highly relevant. Ghironi and Giavazzi claim that a linking of exchange parities (in the form of an EMS-style regime) is preferable to a flexible exchange rate regime. Moreover, as most of the previous authors whose papers are reviewed here, Ghironi and Giavazzi assert that the ability to use fiscal policies to react to supply-side shocks makes all parties better off; therefore, they argue against the rigid application of strict fiscal rules.

The papers summarized in this book testify to the immense interest that the EMU's imminence has generated in the profession. But they also prove the vitality of Mundell's seminal paper. Although Mundell's paper was written 35 years ago, all the papers reviewed here demonstrate that his seminal article has remained the central organizer of ideas and thoughts about monetary integration. Moreover, Mundell's update (in Chapter 2 of this book) is certain to be regarded as another important piece in completing the analytical framework needed to assess correctly the implications and consequences of what has now become the most important project for European, and thus global, monetary and financial markets.

References

Corden, W. M., "European Monetary Union: The Intellectual Prehistory" in Giovannini, A., M. Guitian, and R. Portes, editors, *The Monetary Future of Europe*, Centre for Economic Policy Research (London, 1993).

Eichengreen, B., "European Monetary Unification," *Journal of Economic Literature*, Vol.XXXI, No. 3 (September 1993), pp. 1321–57.

Kenen, P.B., *Economic and Monetary Union in Europe: Moving Beyond Maastricht* (Cambridge University Press, 1995), p. 81.

Tabellini, G. and T. Persson, "Monetary Cohabitation in Europe," NBER Working Paper 5532 (Cambridge: April 1996).

2

Contributions
of
Robert A. Mundell

A Theory of Optimum Currency Areas

Robert A. Mundell*
American Economic Review, 1961

IT IS PATENTLY OBVIOUS THAT PERIODIC BALANCE-OF-PAYMENTS CRISES will remain an integral feature of the international economic system as long as fixed exchange rates and rigid wage and price levels prevent the terms of trade from fulfilling a natural role in the adjustment process. It is, however, far easier to pose the problem and to criticize the alternatives than it is to offer constructive and feasible suggestions for the elimination of what has become an international disequilibrium system.1 The present paper, unfortunately, illustrates that proposition by cautioning against the practicability, in certain cases, of the most plausible alternative: a system of national currencies connected by flexible exchange rates.

A system of flexible exchange rates is usually presented, by its proponents,2 as a device whereby depreciation can take the place of unemployment when the external balance is in deficit, and appreciation can replace inflation when it is in surplus. But the question then arises whether all existing national currencies should be flexible. Should the Ghanian pound be freed to fluctuate against all currencies or ought the present sterling-area currencies remain pegged to the pound sterling? Or, supposing that the Common Market countries proceed with their plans for economic union, should these countries allow each national currency to fluctuate, or would a single currency area be preferable?

The problem can be posed in a general and more revealing way by defining a currency area as a domain within which exchange rates are

---

*The author is an economist in the Special Research Section of the International Monetary Fund.
1I have analyzed this system in some detail in [7].
2See, for example [1], [3], and [5].

fixed and asking: What is the appropriate domain of a currency area? It might seem at first that the question is purely academic since it hardly appears within the realm of political feasibility that national currencies would ever be abandoned in favor of any other arrangement. To this, three answers can be given: (1) Certain parts of the world are undergoing processes of economic integration and disintegration, new experiments are being made, and a conception of what constitutes an optimum currency area can clarify the meaning of these experiments. (2) Those countries, like Canada, which have experimented with flexible exchange rates are likely to face particular problems that the theory of *optimum* currency areas can elucidate if the national currency area does not coincide with the optimum currency area. (3) The idea can be used to illustrate certain functions of currencies that have been inadequately treated in the economic literature and that are sometimes neglected in the consideration of problems of economic policy.

I. Currency Areas and Common Currencies

A single currency implies a single central bank (with note-issuing powers) and therefore a potentially elastic supply of interregional means of payment. But in a currency area comprising more than one currency the supply of international means of payment is conditional upon the cooperation of many central banks; no central bank can expand its own liabilities much faster than other central banks without losing reserves and impairing convertibility.[3] This means that there will be a major difference between adjustment within a currency area that has a single currency and a currency area involving more than one currency; in other words there will be a difference between interregional adjustment and international adjustment even though exchange rates, in the latter case, are fixed.

To illustrate this difference consider a simple model of two entities (regions or countries), initially in full employment and balance-of-payments equilibrium, and see what happens when this equilibrium is disturbed by a shift of demand from the goods of entity B to the goods of entity A. Assume that money wages and prices cannot be reduced in the short run without causing unemployment, and that monetary authorities act to prevent inflation.

Suppose first that the entities are countries with national currencies. The shift of demand from B to A causes unemployment in B and inflationary pressure in A.[4] To the extent that prices are allowed to rise in A

---

[3]More exactly, the rates at which central banks can expand monetary liabilities depend on income elasticities of demand and output elasticities of supply.
[4]For present purposes, inflation is defined as a rise in the prices of home-produced goods.

the change in the terms of trade will relieve B of some of the burden of adjustment. But if A tightens credit restrictions to prevent prices from rising all the burden of adjustment is thrust onto country B; what is needed is a reduction in B's real income and if this cannot be effected by a change in the terms of trade—because B cannot lower, and A will not raise, prices—it must be accomplished by a decline in B's output and employment. The policy of surplus countries in restraining prices therefore imparts a recessive tendency to the world economy on fixed exchange rates or (more generally) to a currency area with many separate currencies.[5]

Contrast this situation with that where the entities are regions within a closed economy lubricated by a common currency; and suppose now that the national government pursues a full-employment policy. The shift of demand from B to A causes unemployment in region B and inflationary pressure in region A, and a surplus in A's balance of payments.[6] To correct the unemployment in B the monetary authorities increase the money supply. The monetary expansion, however, aggravates inflationary pressure in region A: indeed, the principal way in which the monetary policy is effective in correcting full employment in the deficit region is by raising prices in the surplus region, turning the terms of trade against B. Full employment thus imparts an inflationary bias to the multiregional economy or (more generally) to a currency area with common currency.

In a currency area comprising different countries with national currencies the pace of employment in deficit countries is set by the willingness of surplus countries to inflate. But in a currency area comprising many regions and a single currency, the pace of inflation is set by the willingness of central authorities to allow unemployment in deficit regions.

The two systems could be brought closer together by an institutional change: unemployment could be avoided in the world economy if central banks agreed that the burden of international adjustment should fall on surplus countries, which would then inflate until unemployment in deficit countries is eliminated; or a world central bank could be established with power to create an international means of payment. But a currency area of either type cannot prevent both unemployment and inflation among its members. The fault lies not with the type of currency

---

[5]The tendency of surplus countries to control (what is, from a national point of view) inflation can be amply documented from U. S. and French policy in the 1920s and West German policy today. But it is unfortunate that a simple change in world relative prices is interpreted, in the surplus countries, as inflation.

[6]Instructive examples of balance-of-payments problems between different regions of the United States can be found in [2, Ch. 14]. For purposes of this paper regions are defined as areas within which there is factor mobility, but between which there is factor immobility.

area, but with the domain of the currency area. The optimum currency area is not the world.

II. National Currencies and Flexible Exchange Rates

The existence of more than one currency area in the world implies (by definition) variable exchange rates. In the international trade example, if demand shifts from the products of country B to the products of country A, a depreciation by country B or an appreciation by country A would correct the external imbalance and also relieve unemployment in country B and restrain inflation in country A. This is the most favorable case for flexible rates based on national currencies.

Other examples, however, might be equally relevant. Suppose that the world consists of two countries, Canada and the United States, each of which has separate currencies. Also, assume that the continent is divided into two regions that do not correspond to national boundaries—the East, which produces goods like cars, and the West, which produces goods like lumber products. To test the flexible-exchange-rate-argument in this example, assume that the United States dollar fluctuates relative to the Canadian dollar, and that an increase in productivity (say) in the automobile industry causes an excess demand for lumber products and an excess supply of cars.

The immediate impact of the shift in demand is to cause unemployment in the East and inflationary pressure in the West, and a flow of bank reserves from the East to the West because of the former's regional balance-of-payments deficit. To relieve the unemployment in the East, the central banks in both countries would have to expand the national money supplies, or to prevent inflation in the West, contract the national money supplies. (Meanwhile the Canada-United States exchange rate would move to preserve equilibrium in the national balances.) Thus, unemployment can be prevented in both countries, but only at the expense of inflation; or, inflation can be restrained in both countries but at the expense of unemployment; or, finally, the burden of adjustment can be shared between East and West with some unemployment in the East and some inflation in the West. But both unemployment and inflation cannot be escaped. The flexible exchange rate system does not serve to correct the balance-of-payments situation between the two regions (which is the essential problem) although it will do so between the two countries; it is therefore not necessarily preferable to a common currency or national currencies connected by fixed exchange rates.

III. Regional Currency Areas and Flexible Exchange Rates

The preceding example does not destroy the argument for flexible exchange rates, but it might severely impair the relevance of the argument if it is applied to national currencies. The logic of the argument can in fact be rescued if national currencies are abandoned in favor of regional currencies.

To see this, suppose that the "world" reorganizes currencies so that Eastern and Western dollars replace Canadian and U. S. dollars. Now if the exchange rate between the East and the West were pegged, a dilemma would arise similar to that discussed in the first section. But if the East-West exchange rate were flexible, then an excess demand for lumber products need cause neither inflation nor unemployment in either region. The Western dollar appreciates relative to the Eastern dollar thus assuring balance-of-payments equilibrium, while the Eastern and Western central banks adopt monetary policies to ensure constancy of effective demand in terms of the regional currencies, and therefore stable prices and employment.

The same argument could be approached from another direction. A system of flexible exchange rates was originally propounded as an alternative to the gold-standard mechanism that many economists blamed for the worldwide spread of depression after 1929. But if the arguments against the gold standard were correct, then why should a similar argument not apply against a common currency system in a multiregional country? Under the gold standard, depression in one country would be transmitted, through the foreign-trade multiplier, to foreign countries. Similarly, under a common currency, depression in one region would be transmitted to other regions for precisely the same reasons. If the gold standard imposed a harsh discipline on the national economy and induced the transmission of economic fluctuations, then a common currency would be guilty of the same charges; interregional balance-of-payments problems are invisible, so to speak, precisely because there is no escape from the self-adjusting effects of interregional money flows. (It is true, of course, that interregional liquidity can always be supplied by the national central bank, whereas the gold standard and even the gold-exchange standard were hampered, on occasion, by periodic scarcities of internationally liquid assets; but the basic argument against the gold standard was essentially distinct from the liquidity problem.)

Today, if the case for flexible exchange rates is a strong one, it is, in logic, a case for flexible exchange rates based on *regional* currencies, not on national currencies. The optimum currency area is the region.

IV. A Practical Application

The theory of international trade was developed on the Ricardian assumption that factors of production are mobile internally but immobile internationally. Williams, Ohlin, Iversen, and others, however, protested that this assumption was invalid and showed how its relaxation would affect the real theory of trade. I have tried to show that its relaxation has important consequences also for the monetary theory of trade and especially the theory of flexible exchange rates. The argument for flexible exchange rates based on national currencies is only as valid as the Ricardian assumption about factor mobility. If factor mobility is high internally and low internationally a system of flexible exchange rates based on national currencies might work effectively enough. But if regions cut across national boundaries or if countries are multiregional then the argument for flexible exchange rates is only valid if currencies are reorganized on a regional basis.

In the real world, of course, currencies are mainly an expression of national sovereignty, so that actual currency reorganization would be feasible only if it were accompanied by profound political changes. The concept of an optimum currency area therefore has direct practical applicability only in areas where political organization is in a state of flux, such as in ex-colonial areas and in Western Europe.

In Western Europe the creation of the Common Market is regarded by many as an important step toward eventual political union, and the subject of a common currency for the six countries has been much discussed. One can cite the well-known position of J. E. Meade [4, pp. 385–86], who argues that the conditions for a common currency in Western Europe do not exist, and that, especially because of the lack of labor mobility, a system of flexible exchange rates would be more effective in promoting balance-of-payments equilibrium and internal stability; and the apparently opposite view of Tibor Scitovsky [9, Ch. 2],[7] who favors a common currency because he believes that it would induce a greater degree of capital mobility, but further adds that steps must be taken to make labor more mobile and to facilitate supranational employment policies. In terms of the language of this paper, Meade favors national currency areas while Scitovsky gives qualified approval to the idea of a single currency area in Western Europe.

In spite of the apparent contradiction between these two views, the concept of optimum currency areas helps us to see that the conflict reduces to an empirical rather than a theoretical question. In both cases it is implied that an essential ingredient of a common currency, or a single currency area, is a high degree of factor mobility; but Meade believes that the necessary factor mobility does not exist, while Scitovsky argues that labor mobility must be improved and that the creation of a common

---

[7]These statements, of course, cannot do full justice to the arguments of Meade and Scitovsky.

currency would itself stimulate capital mobility. In other words neither writer disputes that the optimum currency area is the region—defined in terms of internal factor mobility and external factor immobility—but there is an implicit difference in views on the precise degree of factor mobility required to delineate a region. The question thus reduces to whether or not Western Europe can be considered a single region, and this is essentially an empirical problem.

V. Upper Limits on the Number of Currencies and Currency Areas

A dilemma now arises: factor mobility (and hence the delineation of regions) is most usefully considered a relative rather than an absolute concept, with both geographical and industrial dimensions, and it is likely to change over time with alterations in political and economic conditions. If, then, the goals of internal stability are to be rigidly pursued, it follows that the greater is the number of separate currency areas in the world, the more successfully will these goals be attained (assuming, as always, that the basic argument for flexible exchange rates per se is valid). But this seems to imply that regions ought to be defined so narrowly as to count every minor pocket of unemployment arising from labor immobility as a separate region, each of which should apparently have a separate currency!

Such an arrangement hardly appeals to common sense. The suggestion reflects the fact that we have, thus far, considered the reasons for keeping currency areas small, not the reasons for maintaining or increasing their size. In other words we have discussed only the stabilization argument, to which end it is preferable to have many currency areas, and not the increasing costs that are likely to be associated with the maintenance of many currency areas.

It will be recalled that the older economists of the nineteenth century were internationalists and generally favored a world currency. Thus, John Stuart Mill wrote [6, p. 176]:

> . . . So much of barbarism, however, still remains in the transactions of most civilized nations, that almost all independent countries choose to assert their nationality by having, to their own inconvenience and that of their neighbors, a peculiar currency of their own.

Mill, like Bagehot and others, was concerned with the costs of valuation and money-changing, not stabilization policy, and it is readily seen that these costs tend to increase with the number of currencies. Any given money qua numeraire or unit of account fulfills this function less adequately if the prices of foreign goods are expressed in terms of foreign currency and must then be translated into domestic currency prices.

Similarly, money in its role of medium of exchange is less useful if there are many currencies; although the costs of currency conversion are always present, they loom exceptionally large under inconvertibility or flexible exchange rates. (Indeed, in a hypothetical world in which the number of currencies equaled the number of commodities, the usefulness of money in its roles of unit of account and medium of exchange would disappear, and trade might just as well be conducted in terms of pure barter.) Money is a convenience and this restricts the optimum number of currencies. In terms of this argument alone the optimum currency area is the world, regardless of the number of regions of which it is composed.

There are two other factors that would inhibit the creation of an arbitrarily large number of currency areas. In the first place markets for foreign exchange must not be so thin that any single speculator (perhaps excepting central banks) can affect the market price; otherwise the speculation argument against flexible exchange rates would assume weighty dimensions. The other argument limiting "balkanization" concerns the very pillar on which the flexible exchange-rate argument rests. The thesis of those who favor flexible exchange rates is that the community in question is not willing to accept variations in its real income through adjustments in its money wage rate or price level, but that it is willing to accept virtually the same changes in its real income through variations in the rate of exchange. In other words it is assumed that unions bargain for a money rather than a real wage, and adjust their wage demands to changes in the cost of living, if at all, only if the cost-of-living index excludes imports. Now, as the currency area grows smaller and the proportion of imports in total consumption grows, this assumption becomes increasingly unlikely. It may not be implausible to suppose that there is some degree of money illusion in the bargaining process between unions and management (or frictions and lags having the same effects), but it is unrealistic to assume the extreme degree of money illusion that would have to exist in small currency areas. Since the necessary degree of money illusion becomes greater the smaller are currency areas, it is plausible to conclude that this also imposes an upper limit on the number of currency areas.

VI. Concluding Argument

The subject of flexible exchange rates can logically be separated into two distinct questions. The first is whether a system of flexible exchange rates can work effectively and efficiently in the modern world economy. For this to be possible it must be demonstrated that: (1) an international price system based on flexible exchange rates is dynamically stable after taking speculative demands into account; (2) the exchange rate changes necessary to eliminate normal disturbances to dynamic equilibrium are not so large as to cause violent and reversible shifts between export- and import-competing industries (this is not ruled out by stability); (3) the risks created by variable exchange rates can be covered at reasonable costs in the forward markets; (4) central banks will refrain from monopolistic speculation; (5) monetary discipline will be maintained by the unfavorable political consequences of continuing depreciation, as it is to some extent maintained today by threats to the levels of foreign exchange reserves; (6) reasonable protection of debtors and creditors can be assured to maintain an increasing flow of long-term capital movements; and (7) wages and profits are not tied to a price index in which import goods are heavily weighted. I have not explicitly discussed these issues in my paper.

The second question concerns how the world should be divided into currency areas. I have argued that the stabilization argument for flexible exchange rates is valid only if it is based on regional currency areas. If the world can be divided into regions within each of which there is factor mobility and between which there is factor immobility, then each of these regions should have a separate currency that fluctuates relative to all other currencies. This carries the argument for flexible exchange rates to its logical conclusion.

But a region is an economic unit while a currency domain is partly an expression of national sovereignty. Except in areas where national sovereignty is being given up it is not feasible to suggest that currencies should be reorganized; the validity of the argument for flexible exchange rates therefore hinges on the closeness with which nations correspond to regions. The argument works best if each nation (and currency) has internal factor mobility and external factor immobility. But if labor and capital are insufficiently mobile within a country, then flexibility of the external price of the national currency cannot be expected to perform the stabilization function attributed to it, and one could expect varying rates of unemployment or inflation in the different regions. Similarly, if factors are mobile across national boundaries then a flexible exchange system becomes unnecessary, and may even be positively harmful, as I have suggested elsewhere.[8]

---

[8]In my paper, "The Monetary Dynamics of International Adjustment under Fixed and Flexible Exchange Rates," [8], I advanced the argument that stabilization policy would be more difficult under fixed exchange rates if short-term capital were immobile than if it were mobile, and more difficult under flexible exchange rates if capital were mobile than if it were immobile. Although the method of analysis was fundamentally different the conclusions support the hypothesis of this paper that the fixed-exchange-rate system is better within areas where factors are mobile and the flexible-exchange-rate system is better for areas between which factors are immobile. The argument of my other paper imposes an additional argument against increasing the number of currencies.

Canada provides the only modern example where an advanced country has experimented with flexible exchange rates. According to my argument the experiment should be largely unsuccessful as far as stabilization is concerned. Because of the factor immobility between regions an increase in foreign demand for the products of one of the regions would cause an appreciation of the exchange rate and therefore increased unemployment in the remaining regions, a process that could be corrected by a monetary policy that aggravated inflationary pressures in the first region; every change in demand for the products in one region is likely to induce opposite changes in other regions that cannot be entirely modified by national stabilization policies. Similarly the high degree of external capital mobility is likely to interfere with stabilization policy for completely different reasons: to achieve internal stability the central bank can alter credit conditions, but it is the change in the exchange rate rather than the alteration in the interest rate that produces the stabilizing effect; this indirectness conduces to a cyclical approach to equilibrium. Although an explicit empirical study would be necessary to verify that the Canadian experiment has not fulfilled the claims made for flexible exchange rates, the prima facie evidence indicates that it has not. It must be emphasized, though, that a failure of the Canadian experiment would cast doubt only on the effectiveness of a flexible exchange system in a multiregional country, not on a flexible exchange system in a unitary country.[9]

References

Friedman, M., "The Case for Flexible Exchange Rates," *Essays in Positive Economics* (Chicago 1953).

Harris, S.E., *Interregional and International Economics* (New York 1957).

Lutz, L., "The Case for Flexible Exchange Rates," Banca Naz. del Lavoro (December 1954).

Meade, J.E., "The Balance of Payments Problems of a Free Trade Area," *Economic Journal*, (September 1957), 67, pp. 379–96.

————, "The Case for Variable Exchange Rates," Three Banks Review (Sept. 1955).

Mill, J. S., *Principles of Political Economy*, Vol. II (New York, 1894).

Mundell, R.A., "The International Disequilibrium System," *Kyklos* (1961) 2, 14, pp. 153–72.

————, "The Monetary Dynamics of International Adjustment under Fixed and Flexible Exchange Rates," *Quarterly Journal of Economics* (May 1960), 74, pp. 227–57.

---

[9]Other economists have advanced arguments in favor of balkanization of multiregional countries (see for example, A. D. Scott [10]); and the argument for regional currency areas adds to the list; but, as Scott is careful to emphasize, no country can make such decisions on purely economic grounds.

Scitovsky, T., *Economic Theory and Western European Integration* (Stanford, 1958).

Scott, A.D., "A Note on Grants in Federal Countries," *Economica* (November 1950), 17 (N.S.), pp. 416–22.

Updating the Agenda for Monetary Union

Robert A. Mundell*

T ODAY, THIRTY FIVE YEARS AFTER THE PUBLICATION of my 1961 article on optimum currency areas (OCA), I would like to describe how the article came about, my intentions when I wrote it, and then comment on the current relevance of the subject.

Genesis of the Article

The beginnings of the idea first occurred to me in the academic year 1955–56, when I was writing my dissertation under James Meade for the Massachusetts Institute for Technology (MIT) at the London School of Economics (LSE). My dissertation for MIT, entitled "Essays on the Theory of Capital Movements," was devoted entirely to the real side of the subject—the transfer problem, stability conditions, welfare implications, factor mobility, transport costs, and so on; it had nothing to do with flexible or fixed exchange rates. Meade, however, was an ardent advocate of flexible exchange rates and it was a hot subject at LSE. He had suggested that the signers of the Treaty of Rome achieve balance of payments equilibrium by letting exchange rates float. At that time, I had an open mind on the subject, but I could not see why countries in the process of forming a common market should saddle themselves with a new barrier to exchange in the form of uncertainty about exchange rates.

*An extended version of a luncheon speech presented at the December 1996 Tel Aviv conference on optimum currency areas.

In the next academic year, 1956–57, I was a post-doctoral fellow in political economy at the University of Chicago. Milton Friedman, like Meade, championed flexible exchange rates, but for very different reasons. Meade, the liberal socialist, saw flexible rates as a device for achieving external balance while freeing policy tools for the implementation of national planning objectives. Friedman, the libertarian conservative, saw flexible exchange rates as a way of getting rid of exchange and trade controls. Both economists saw flexible rates as a means of altering real wages when money wage rigidities would otherwise cause unemployment. The analogy frequently used was that it was easier to put the clocks back than change people's habits.

As at LSE, flexible exchange rates was a hot topic at Chicago, billed as a free market alternative to fixed exchange rates. It occurred to me that if the case for flexible exchange rates held for the United States or Canada, it should also hold for any of the regions within these two multiregional countries. But to have flexible exchange rates between regions of the same country, it would be necessary to have more than one currency. Were there not costs associated with creating additional currencies? Milton's answer was that if the argument for regional currencies was correct within a particular country, it was probably becoming less important as the national economy became more integrated. The upshot, however, was that I began thinking seriously about the relationship between "regions" and "countries" in the context of monetary systems.

Students of trade theory were aware of the criticism that John H. Williams had made of the classical model of trade, based on the supposition that factors of production were mobile internally but immobile internationally. Williams argued that factors were by no means completely mobile within countries, nor completely immobile between countries. Once said, this is obvious, as any glance at history will confirm. But, despite the work of Bertil Ohlin and especially Carl Iversen—who took explicit account of factor movements—the theory of trade typically identified regions with countries. I began to see that the same criticism that Williams had made of real trade theory might apply to international monetary theory and the theory of exchange rates.

In 1957, I returned to Canada to teach at the University of British Columbia. In the fall of that year, I presented a paper at a faculty seminar on flexible exchange rates and regional problems. In the paper, I introduced the idea that if the theory of flexible exchange rates endorsed by James Meade and Milton Friedman were valid, it would apply to British Columbia and the other individual regions within Canada rather than to Canada itself. The Canadian dollar, which, uniquely among the currencies of the Group of Ten countries was then floating, had not helped Canada escape the U.S. business cycle; in any case, it was aimed at the stability of the heartland economy of Ontario and lower Quebec and not at the peripheral regions in the west, the north, and the Maritimes. I also noted that Canadian labor unions were not independent of U.S. labor unions so that even though the Canadian dollar had appreciated against the U.S. dollar, wage expansion was no slower in Canada than in the United States. I was not, however, proposing an independent currency for British Columbia; rather, I was beginning to think of the argument as a qualification, if not a refutation, of the argument for flexible exchange rates.

I spent the next academic year, 1958–59, at Stanford University. By this time, I had developed what would become known as the "Mundell-Fleming model." At Stanford, I presented a paper at a faculty seminar entitled something like "The Theory of International Adjustment and Optimum Currency Units." This was the first public presentation of my external-internal balance dynamic model (Mundell, May 1960), and I was flattered to have in my audience not just Lorie Tarshis, Ed Shaw, Ken Arrow, Bernard Haley and Mel Reder and others from Stanford, but also Abba Lerner and Tibor Scitovsky from Berkeley. I spent most of my time at the seminar explaining the dynamic model and the adjustment mechanism under fixed and flexible exchange rates. After the seminar, Lerner chided me for not having talked enough about optimum currency areas, but with his great intellect, it was easy for him to grasp my basic idea in a few sentences. After that seminar, I submitted a long paper to Roy Harrod, editor of the *Economic Journal.* I included in it not only the model of monetary and exchange rate dynamics, but also the theory of international disequilibrium, the appropriate mix of monetary and fiscal policy for internal and external balance, the principle of effective market classification, and the theory of optimum currency areas.

When Harrod rejected it, I was naturally disappointed, but, in retrospect, he did me a favor. The rejection taught me not to overload an article with too many ideas. The Tinbergenian principle is a good rule of thumb here as in economic policy: one target, one instrument; one idea, one paper!

I spent the next two years, 1959–61, at the Bologna Center of The Johns Hopkins School of Advanced International Studies, where I put the finishing touches on my optimum currency area paper. I remember a precocious student there, Helmuth Mayer (who went on to a career at the Bank for International Settlements and became an expert on the Eurodollar market), helping me decide whether to call the paper "Optimum Currency Units" or "Optimum Currency Areas." The next question was where to send it. I had already published two articles in the *American Economic Review* (Mundell: 1957, 1960), another in the *Quarterly Journal of Economics* (Mundell, 1960), and another two in the

Canadian Journal of Economics and Political Science (Mundell: 1957, 1961). So I sent the article to *Economica*. When it was rejected, I sent it to the *AER,* where Bernard Haley enthusiastically accepted it. It came out in September 1961 (Mundell, November 1961).

Doubts About Flexible Exchange Rates

The story of the *idea* did not end with the article. My own views evolved and the issue became a subject of discussion in the literature. The article presented a qualification to the case for flexible exchange rates, which—provided the basic argument was valid—works best when currency areas are regions. I spent the next two years, 1961–63, at the IMF. There I was involved mainly with the theory of the policy mix, the theory of inflation, and the monetary approach to the balance of payments. There was not much to report on optimum currency areas, except that I tried—unsuccessfully—to get the IMF to address the optimum currency area issue in the case against flexible exchange rates, which the staff was preparing for its 1962 Annual Report.

At this point, I was skeptical about the applicability of flexible exchange rates in many situations, but not opposed as a matter of principle. My testimony to the Joint Economic Committee in 1963 (Mundell, 1963) reveals that at that time I was still rather sympathetic to the use of exchange rates as a mechanism of adjustment. But my main interest was in getting the arguments right. Starting in 1964, I took part in the Bellagio-Princeton Study Group on International Monetary Reform, organized by Fritz Machlup, Robert Triffin, and William Fellner. This group distinguished four main options for the international monetary system: the gold standard; flexible exchange rates; a new international reserve facility; and a world central bank.

Following up those discussions was a petition in 1966 urging the generalized adoption of flexible exchange rates. When I failed to respond to the petition, Willy Fellner called to ask whether my nonresponse indicated an objection. I told him, yes, that I had concluded that a movement to generalized flexible exchange rates would be a step backward for the international monetary system. It was with great regret that I felt compelled to distance myself on this basic policy issue from such teachers and good friends as James Meade, Milton Friedman, Harry Johnson, Gottfried Haberler, Fritz Machlup, Lloyd Metzler and Arnold Harberger, and others who supported flexible exchange rates. I found myself in such diverse company as Lord Robbins, Sir Roy Harrod, Jacques Rueff, Edward Bernstein, Robert Triffin, Otmar Emminger, Rinaldo Ossola, Charles Kindleberger, Guido Carli, and Robert Roosa—and some of them would later become defectors. Of course, I was happy to be in the company of great economists of the past who, with the possible exceptions of Fisher and Keynes, were vigorously opposed to flexible exchange rates between countries with inconvertible currencies.

Like the tariff and bimetallic controversies of the late nineteenth century, the flexible exchange rate controversy was complicated by considerations far beyond economics as it was normally conceived. From a theoretical point of view, I had come to have strong doubts about the validity of the basic argument for flexible exchange rates as an adjustment mechanism, and became more appreciative of the adjustment mechanism under fixed exchange rates. It was not that I had forgotten the Mundell-Fleming model; rather, I had gone beyond it.

The choice between fixed and flexible exchange rates is a false and biased way of posing the issue. It conveys the false suggestion that flexibility of the exchange rate provides an extra degree of freedom. In a general equilibrium system, there is one degree of freedom; how it is used characterizes the system. A country has a choice to stabilize such possible targets as the price level, the money supply, the exchange rate, the price of gold, or the wage rate. In other words, it can have a commodity standard, a monetary standard, a foreign currency standard, a gold standard, or a wage standard. In the international monetary system of the 1960s, the price of gold was fixed by the United States, and the price of the dollar was fixed by foreign countries. Moving toward flexible exchange rates (and a flexible price of gold for the United States) shifts the burden of stabilization policy onto a monetary standard (a là Friedman), a commodity standard (a là Thomas Attwood, Irving Fisher, or Frank Graham), or a wage standard. Four main possibilities are as follows:

"Standard"	Fixed Target	Variable	Variable	Variable
Commodity	price level	exchange rate	money supply	gold price
Monetary	money supply	exchange rate	price level	gold price
Foreign Currency	exchange rate	money supply	price level	gold price
Gold	gold price	money supply	exchange rate	price level

When the issue is posed in this way, one variable is fixed and three are flexible; there is no extra degree of freedom in the framework of a stable system. Of course, the authorities could choose not to fix any single variable but instead to fix a weighted average of the price level, the money supply, the exchange rate, and the price of gold. Even in this case, however, there is no extra degree of freedom.

My objections to flexible exchange rates exclude two very different types of cases. Very unstable countries—usually the result of large budget deficits financed by the banking system—cannot have fixed exchange rates; in general, a country that is inflating relative to its currency-area partner cannot maintain fixed exchange rates. Nor do the objections apply to a very large country in a world without an established international monetary system. The largest economy in the world—the United States—does not have the option of fixing exchange rates unilaterally.

Initial conditions matter. In the 1960s, there was a coherent international monetary system even if it had developed problems arising from the undervaluation of gold. There were definite costs to abandoning the system.

Apart from that, I had come to doubt the basic arguments for flexible exchange rates. First, I came to doubt the validity of the money-illusion argument for flexible exchange rates. Already in my OCA paper, I had argued that exchange flexibility would not work in small open currency areas because to be effective it would require an unrealistic degree of money illusion. Moreover, money illusion is affected by experience. The more inflation a country experiences, the more it is built into expectations, and the more unions try to insert inflation premiums into wage demands. The first devaluation may work without too much inflation; the second invites a wage response; and the third provokes compensation demands. Keynes hit it on the nose when he said that employment might be governed by a monetary policy conducted by the trade unions instead of by the banking system!

One can understand why a generation of economists brought up in the great depression could believe in money illusion. In the early 1930s, the public of most countries (except those that had experienced hyperinflation in the post-war period) had come to expect deflation, or at least price stability. With mass unemployment, and a history of gold-standard stability or deflation, people would not worry too much about inflation, which, in any case, was thought of in some quarters as a way of bailing out debtors and as an antidote to the depression. But three decades after the great depression, a full generation had grown up knowing only inflation. It took some time before the real-world lesson of inflation set in—students take their biases as well as their models from their teachers—but eventually new premises spring forward; as Paul Samuelson, paraphrasing Max Planck, once put it, science progresses funeral by funeral.

Second, my continued study of the adjustment mechanism encouraged my optimism about the ease of adjustment under fixed exchange rates. I recall Taussig's astonishment when he reviewed the evidence of his students—Jacob Viner, John Williams, Harry Dexter White, and others—on the transfer problem. He was stunned by how quickly and easily current accounts adjusted to capital movements; even if the terms of trade or relative price levels change in the direction predicted by classical theory, the changes were too small to have been responsible for the recorded shifts in trade balances. Taussig's objectivity opened the way to the rediscovery by Bertil Ohlin of expenditure effects—rediscovery because a host of early writers, including Gervaise, Thornton, Ricardo, Bastable, and Wicksell, were aware of them—which greatly expedited the transfer process. In addition, the classical constant-purchasing-power model needed to be supplemented by money-induced expenditure effects. When both of these effects are incorporated into the Mundell-Fleming model, international adjustment of the balance of payments becomes much smoother without the necessity of troublesome changes in relative prices, wages, or employment. Inter-regional adjustment of the current account to capital flows occurs without dramatic problems between regions of the same monetary area; why should it be any different between countries under firmly fixed exchange rates?

Of course, one can construct models where a transfer can affect the terms of trade or real exchange rate, and history is replete with exchange rate crises. It is a mistake, however, to blame the fixed exchange rate mechanism for these crises. There is an asymmetry between the pain of adjusting upward and downward. Few countries have problems generating a current account deficit in response to a capital inflow; it is the opposite adjustment that creates the problem. I do not believe now—nor did I in the 1960s—that devaluation is a good way of easing the pain; devaluation adds no new resources except for a possible employment stimulus. As Mexico's experience after 1976 or 1994 confirms, devaluation starts the inflation cycle all over again.

A third reason for my doubting flexible exchange rates was that I had come to the conclusion that for many countries a fixed rate system (with its automatic monetary adjustment) was a more effective barrier against inflation than alternatives involving flexible rates. One of the problems is that policy makers choose flexible rates over fixed rates without substituting an alternative stabilization procedure. It is one thing to substitute price-level or money-supply targeting for exchange rate targeting; it is quite another to abandon a fixed rate system without replacing it with an alternative brake.

Fourth, several types of economies of scale are associated with the formation of currency areas. First, there is an economy in policy formation. When a small country fixes its currency to that of a larger country with an acceptable inflation rate, it sets the course for the rest of its macroeconomic policies (an accommodating monetary policy, as well as budget discipline, is required). Thus, when Milton Friedman advised Yugoslavia to fix the dinar to the deutsche mark in the 1970s, he remarked bluntly that Germany had a better monetary policy than

Yugoslavia (Friedman, 1973). Second, there is an economy in size from the standpoint of insulation against shocks; the more countries that join a currency area, the smaller the proportion to its output of any internal or external disturbance. Third, because money is a unit of account, there are economies of information and convenience in fixed exchange rates, compared with flexible exchange rates; and to currency unions, compared with currency areas. The more countries that join a currency area, the more efficient it will be. Indeed, these economies-of-scale factors led to the emergence of one or two precious metals as the base of historical international monetary systems. From the standpoint of these factors, the optimum currency area is the world.

A fifth reason for my doubts about flexible exchange rates owed to my conviction that there was a fundamental asymmetry in the adjustment of large and small countries. I studied the impact of size in three papers in the 1960s. In the first (Mundell, 1964), I elaborated the Mundell-Fleming model to a two-country world; this model showed, among other things, that the multiplier was different for large and small countries. The second paper (Mundell, 1965) demonstrated that under both classical and Keynesian assumptions, the distribution of the burden of adjustment varies inversely with the size of the country. In the third paper (Mundell, 1968), entitled "Gold and the Gulliver Problem," I analyzed international monetary conditions when the world configuration of countries included a superpower, a few "oligops," and many ministates. In this paper, I argued that the oligops would be restive under a dollar standard and would seek to challenge it through a currency alliance of their own, but that this outcome was inferior to the superpower accepting a world currency. I had come to the conclusion, as I argued at the Joint Economic Committee (Mundell, 1968), that a world currency was the theoretical optimum and that as we backtrack from the drafting board toward second-best feasible solutions, we should be aware of the nature of the costs incurred.

I have long believed that the interdependence of exchange rates and balances of payments in the world economy could best be managed multilaterally. It is true that the rest of the world needs an international monetary system much more than the United States. In the absence of an international monetary system, the superpower dominates and bilateral bashing replaces multilateral rules. Although superpower pre-eminence will be apparent even in an international monetary system, there is at least a set of rules that apply equally and a multilateral framework for resolving disputes. The biggest casualty of the breakup of the international monetary system was the plan for European monetary union put into motion at the Hague Summit in 1969. European economies were better integrated around the dollar than in the two decades that followed. When the dollar was taken off gold, the legal basis for the dollar's position at the center of the system ended, and the other major countries went off the dollar. The movement to flexible exchange rates in 1973 made a world of currency areas inevitable.

In December 1975, I presented a paper to the American Geographical Society entitled, "The Geography of Inflation and the Reform of the Gold Standard" (Mundell, 1976), in which I related the geography of inflation to currency areas:

> "...The most important intellectual tool an economist can give a geographer on this subject is the *currency area* concept. If geographers seek iso-inflation zones they can do so by mapping currency areas. In the bimetallic and duo-metallic periods of the 19th century, they need only note shifts of the bimetallic ratio (the price of gold in terms of silver) and the independent inconvertible currencies. Inflation rates differ in the long run because of exchange rate changes. During the Bretton Woods era, the dollar area had a common rate of inflation except when a country abandoned the dollar by devaluation. The dollar area was almost world wide after 1949 and the United States called the tune of world inflation. Exceptions of high inflation areas were always sections of the world where currencies had been devalued or were depreciating. With the breakdown in the international monetary system and more generalized floating exchange rates since 1973, each currency or currency area becomes its own inflation source. The world monetary economy ceased to act as a monetary unit when floating rates were introduced in 1973. Each country floating separately had an independent rate of inflation."

A currency-area map should therefore identify iso-inflation zones.

In the international jungle of independent currency areas, the superpower, as already noted, dominates. The dollar is the main unit for international price quotations, contracts, invoicing, and currency reserves. Floating rates do not reduce the need for international reserves; indeed, foreign exchange reserves as a percent of imports have grown—they totaled 17.4 percent at the end of 1995, compared with 12.3 percent at the end of 1969. This increase in demand makes the United States the main beneficiary and encourages it to adopt a higher "optimal" rate of inflation than it would otherwise (Mundell, 1971). Because of the international demand for its currency, and subject to the constraint imposed by the threat of entry, the United States will have a higher optimal rate of inflation than it would in the absence of the international use of its currency.

The argument for the reserve country applying the inflation tax on the rest of the world should not be exaggerated. Demand for international reserves is not inelastic. If the superpower abuses its monopoly position, the rest of the world can form a defensive league against it and take steps to find alternatives. When, in the late 1970s, the United States went on an irresponsible inflation binge, Europe was provoked into creating the European Monetary System (EMS).

An international monetary system is easier to destroy than to rebuild. It was easy enough for a few amateurs in a few hours to wreck the international monetary system in August 1971. Compare that to the protracted negotiations that went into the Bretton Woods Articles of Agreement. It is not that this agreement created an international monetary system. Rather, it merely devised the set of rules and procedures for making other countries comfortable with the existing system, the anchored dollar standard. The great significance of the agreement lay in its creation of a multilateral way of managing the international interdependence of exchange rates in a forum in which the interests of the smaller countries could be taken into account.

The Unit-of-Account Property of Money

In the last part of my OCA article, I address the issue of money serving as a unit of account, as well as a medium of exchange. We have already discussed the money illusion argument, which requires that currency areas be large; and the economies-of-scale factors that increase with the size of the currency area. There is also the problem of size with respect to the monopoly issue; in this connection, I wrote: "...markets for foreign exchange must not be so thin that any single speculator can affect the market price; otherwise the speculation argument against flexible exchange rates would assume weighty dimensions." In a world of big international banks and multinational corporations, there is not much scope in practice for the monetary independence of any but a few large countries.

From the standpoint of the unit-of-account properties of money, the fewer the currencies the better. After quoting a passage from Mill that identifies national currencies with a form of barbarism, I wrote:

"Mill, like Bagehot and others, was concerned with the costs of valuation and money changing, not stabilization policy, and it is readily seen that these costs tend to increase with the number of currencies. Any given money qua numeraire, or unit of account, fulfills this function less adequately if the prices of foreign goods are expressed in terms of foreign currency and must then be translated into domestic currency prices. Similarly, money in its role of medium of exchange is less useful if there are many currencies; although the costs of currency conversion are always present, they loom exceptionally large under inconvertibility or flexible exchange rates. (Indeed, in a hypothetical world in which the number of currencies equaled the number of commodities, the usefulness of money in its roles of unit of account and medium of exchange would disappear, and trade might just as well be conducted in terms of pure barter.) Money is a convenience and this restricts the optimum number of currencies. In terms of this argument alone, the optimum currency area is the world, regardless of the number of regions of which it is composed."

The unit-of-account property of money has an ancient history in economics, although one not well modeled. The idea of money as a unit of account was known to Aristotle, Plato, and Oresme. But it did not become an important part of economics until late in the seventeenth century, when, during the great debate over recoinage in England in the 1690s, the unit-of-account role crystallized into two extreme views. As background for the debate, the newly formed Bank of England had just issued £1,200,000 in bank notes to the government in return for a large public loan to finance "King Billy's War." An economist today, such as David Hume two and a half centuries earlier, would recognize that this new issue of notes to finance government spending would displace an almost equal amount of specie.

But which specie? Up to that time, coins had been accepted at face value, but a distinction was suddenly made between full-valued and light coins, since they fetched a different price abroad. As Aristophanes and Thomas Gresham would know, the best coins were exported and the worst stayed at home. Coins thus fell toward their metallic value. The pound depreciated by about 25 percent against gold weight and prices began to rise. It was then decided to organize a recoinage and the question was: should coins be put in circulation with a quarter less silver, yet still be called a pound; or should coins with the old silver content be put in circulation to maintain the historical value of the pound? Enter the protagonists: Lowndes, the Secretary of the Treasury, against John Locke, the philosopher, supported by Charles Montagu, the Chancellor of the Exchequer (and later the Earl of Halifax). Newton also participated in the debate, first advocating devaluation and then coming out on the side of the metallists.

Lowndes favored a devaluation to keep prices more or less where they were and to finance the recoinage, recognizing money's role as unit of account. Locke countered with vigorous (if incorrect) logic that money was nothing more nor less than the metallic value of the silver of which it was composed. Thus began the train of thought and controversy between the metallists and the cartalists.

From the standpoint of expediency in dealing with the problem, as well as insight into the nature of money as a token, Lowndes (and Newton in his initial position) was right; from the standpoint of protecting bondholders and long-run stability, Locke (and Newton, in his second position) was right. Logic won over insight, and the newly created heavy coins continued to be exported. But Locke's recipe for maintaining the standard (whether gold or silver) held the day for more than two centuries, resulting in Britain's restoring the standard after the Napoleonic Wars and after World War I.

Keynes took up the issue of money's unit of account role in the 1930s. In the opening of the *Treatise,* he writes: "Money of account, namely, that unit in which debts and prices are expressed, is the primary concept of the theory of money." Money's unit of account role is now embodied in the term "money illusion," which is the concept that money in and of itself takes on its own significance. Since Keynes' writings in 1930, the Lowndes-Keynes view emphasizing the short-run expediency of devaluation and inflation has come to dominate the thinking of policy makers and the international organizations.

Decisions about currency areas should not lose sight of money's unit-of-account role. Purchasing power parity cannot be relied on in the short run between large currency areas. Firmly fixed exchange rates are more conducive to the operation of the law of one price than flexible rates, and monetary unions are more conducive than merely fixed rates. The departure of relative prices from purchasing-power-parity norms should be a wake-up call for those who believe flexible rates are efficient. From the standpoint of the unit-of-account factor, the optimum currency area is the world.

Fixed Rates and the Adjustment Mechanism

There is an important difference between a "fixed" exchange rate and a "pegged" exchange rate. The fixed rate, as I use the term, presupposes that the money supply is allowed to increase and decrease with balance of payments surpluses or deficits, while the pegged rate allows monetary policy to finance budget deficits or to support an inflation rate incompatible with maintenance of the exchange rate. The pegged rate system deserves to be discredited as the worst of all systems, while the fixed rate will be, for many countries, the best of all systems. In the literature, however, much confusion arises out of the failure to distinguish between the two arrangements.

A currency board system has virtually nothing in common with a pegged exchange rate, but it can be seen as a extreme case of a fixed exchange rate system. Under a currency board system, the central bank buys and sells only foreign exchange, maintaining its reserves entirely in foreign exchange or liquid foreign exchange earning assets. It may maintain 100 percent—or even higher—reserves if it establishes a supplementary fund to fulfill a role as lender of last resort to the commercial banks. The key element in a currency board system is that the exchange rate is kept fixed within narrow or zero margins and that the peg can be changed only by parliamentary or constitutional change, which can only be negotiated with great difficulty—thus generating confidence in the continuation of the system. I am glad to see that the IMF is now supporting the idea of currency boards for some countries.

The most important element of any sound monetary system is that monetary policy be predictable. Under a firmly fixed exchange rate system, the key element is that there is little if any expectation of a change in the exchange rate because monetary policy is automatically geared to making the exchange rate an equilibrium rate. A sufficient directive to central banks would be that the central bank deal only in foreign assets within the required margins of the par value. If applied strictly, the reserve base of the money supply could only increase as a result of a balance of payments surplus. (In a large and growing country, with sufficient reserves, some allowance could be made for fiduciary monetary expansion after the public's confidence in the system has been earned.)

In the modern world, we are poles away from the perceptions existing at the time of the Bretton Woods meeting when 44 nations endorsed fixed exchange rates (anchored through the dollar to gold) and rejected the alternative as a form of currency chaos, a throwback to the world of the 1930s to which no country wanted to return. The anchored dollar standard from 1936 to 1971 was by no means as effective an arrangement as the gold standard. It was nevertheless a coherent system and the only one possible under the prevailing circumstances. It provided a satisfactory solution to the problem of inflation convergence, a high level of employment, balance of payments equilibrium, and a tolerable rate of inflation for the world as a whole. To appreciate the commitment to the system by IMF members, one need only read the attacks on the alternative of flexible exchange rates in the IMF Annual Reports of 1950 and 1962.

The perception that world inflation could best be contained by a common approach in the context of an international monetary system changed completely in the 1970s. By that time, three successive secretaries of the U.S. Treasury harbored a bee in their bonnets: flexible-exchange-rate monetarism. This view was championed by the vigorous logic of Milton Friedman, a protagonist just as effective as John Locke. It led to the second amendment of the IMF's Articles of Agreement, endorsing "managed" flexible exchange rates. Ironically, the two European presidents who were partners in the scheme soon changed their minds and signed the agreement that led to the creation of a regional monetary system in Europe. Inevitably, the example of Europe will be followed elsewhere, particularly, but not exclusively, in Asia, as the disintegration of the international monetary system creates a new externality that can be internalized—as a second-best alternative to an international monetary system—by regional monetary arrangements. Why not a monetary system for each continent, or for each civilization?

Not surprisingly, two decades of flexible exchange rates have been too much of a bad thing. Now both fixed and flexible exchange rates have been discredited! Fixed exchange rates have become confused with "pegged" rates. Monetary unions or currency boards, on the other hand,

Spectrum of Exchange Rate Arrangements

System	Monetary Policy	Par Value	Margins
clean float	independent	none	none
dirty float	independent	none	none
sliding-gliding parity or tablita	independent	variable	optional
pegged rates	independent	short-term	optional
fixed exchange rates	adaptive or automatic	long-term	narrow
currency board	adaptive or automatic	long-term	tiny
monetary union	automatic	forever	none

have become respectable. This is a curious thing. Monetary unions and currency boards are eminently respectable, as are flexible exchange rates, but not so fixed exchange rates. The reason is that fixed exchange rates have become tarred with the same feather as "pegged rates," which usually, if not inevitably, leads to one-war speculation and currency crises.

My own view is that a parity system of fixed exchange rates is completely viable as long as the automatic adjustment mechanism is allowed to work itself out. This means no sterilization. We have thriving examples of fixed exchange rate regimes in Austria, Holland, and Belgium (and indirectly Luxembourg), tied to the deutsche mark, and decades of examples of viable fixed exchange rates before the governors of the IMF shifted to flexible rates. The recent example of Argentina's fixed exchange rate system tied to the dollar is an encouraging sign; if allowed to be successful, it will help refute the view that fixed exchange rates cannot work. These, and other examples including successful currency board arrangements, eloquently refute the idea that fixed rate systems cannot work without political integration. The gold standard was a way of organizing a fixed exchange rate system without the need for political integration.

This is not to say that there are no advantages to moving from a currency area to a monetary union. The former is a half-way house that confers many of the benefits of monetary union without the political integration that in the current world is unrealistic, or at least premature. In any case, the best path toward monetary union is through irrevocably fixed exchange rates.

The Case for and Against Joining an OCA

Before listing some criteria justifying a country's fixing the exchange rate to a currency area or monetary union, allow me to list some of the circumstances under which a country might decide *against* joining a fixed exchange rate zone or a currency union:

(1) it wants an inflation rate different from the currency area rate;

(2) it wants to use the exchange rate as an instrument of employment policy to lower or raise wages;

(3) it wants to use the exchange rate as a beggar-thy-neighbor instrument to capture employment from other countries;

(4) as a large country, it does not want an unfriendly country to benefit from the economies-of-size advantages of the large currency area, or because it fears that the addition of another currency will complicate national macroeconomic policy making;

(5) it wants to use the money-expansion or inflation tax to finance government spending, and it would be prevented from doing so to the extent desired by the discipline of fixed exchange rates;

(6) the country—especially if it is large—does not want to sacrifice seigniorage from the use of its money as an international means of payment;

(7) the government wants to use seigniorage as a source of hidden or off-budget funding for personal use by members of a corrupt dictatorship or naive democratic government;

(8) a regime of fixed exchange rates could conflict with the required policies of a central bank that had a constitutional mandate to preserve price stability;

(9) monetary integration with one or more other countries would remove a dimension of national sovereignty that is a vital symbol of national independence;

(10) it wants to optimize the currency denominations appropriate to its per capita income (which would be relevant only in the case of currency unions, not fixed rates);

(11) it wants to maintain monetary independence to use the money-expansion or inflation tax in the event of war;

(12) it wants to protect the secrecy of its statistics, as when the Soviet Union opted out of the IMF and forced its Eastern European satellites to do the same;

(13) there is no domestic political and economic leadership capable of maintaining a fixed exchange rate system in equilibrium;

(14) the political authorities cannot achieve budget balance and/or establish confidence in the permanence of budgetary equilibrium or the viability of fixed exchange rates;

(15) the partners in the prospective currency area are politically unstable or prone to invasion by aggressor countries;

(16) the partner countries are poorer and will expect, aid, "equalization payments," or otherwise an unduly large proportion of the OCA's expenditures; and

(17) it does not want to accept the degree of integration implied by the OCA agreement, such as common standards, immigration, labor, or tax legislation.

So much for the case against joining an OCA. The following are some of the reasons why a country might instead choose to join an OCA:

(1) to gain the inflation rate of the OCA;

(2) to reduce transactions costs in trade with a major partner;

(3) to eliminate the cost of printing and maintaining a separate national currency;

(4) to participate in a purchasing power parity area, which would be fostered by fixed exchange rates and even more by monetary union;

(5) to establish an anchor for policy, a fixed point around which expectations can be formulated and policies can revolve;

(6) to remove discretion from monetary and fiscal policy authorities;

(7) to keep the exchange rate from being kicked around as a political football by vested interests that want depreciation to boost profits or to bail out debtors;

(8) to establish an automatic mechanism to enforce monetary and fiscal discipline;

(9) to have a multinational cushion against shocks;

(10) to participate more fully and on more equal terms in the financial center and capital market of the union;

(11) to provide a catalyst for political alliance or integration;

(12) to establish a power bloc as a countervailing influence against the domination of neighboring powers;

(13) to share in the political decision of determining the OCA's inflation rate;

(14) to establish a competing international currency as a rival to the dollar and earn, instead of pay, seigniorage;

(15) to reinforce or establish an economic power bloc that will have more clout in international economic discussions and have greater power to improve, by its trade policy, its terms of trade;

(16) to delegate to a mechanism outside the domestic political process the enforcement of monetary and fiscal discipline; and

(17) to participate in restoring a reformed world monetary system.

The Viability of EMU

With respect to my position on European economic and monetary union (EMU), I have already put my cards on the table. I began thinking about this issue when I was at the Bologna Center in 1959–61. I remember my complete agreement when Lionel Robbins, on one of his annual visits to the Center, told me that he had come to the conclusion that a European currency was both viable and desirable. In my booklet (Mundell, 1965), I analyzed a model of three currency areas—the dollar area, the sterling area, and a third bloc based on a European currency, which I called the "thaler" area. At that time, there was not much enthusiasm for a European currency, but by the late 1960s things had changed. In 1969, I presented a paper in New York called "The Case for a European Currency" (Mundell, 1969), which was widely reported in Europe. It contained my proposal for a European currency, which I dubbed the "europa." A revised version of this paper entitled "A Plan for a European Currency" (Mundell, 1973), was presented at the Conference on Optimum Currency Areas in Madrid in March 1970. My 1969 paper led to an invitation to come to Brussels to prepare alternative plans for a European currency the following summer, which I was able to do en route to Addis Ababa to prepare a report on currency problems in Africa (Mundell: 1970, 1972).

I see two recent changes in the winds regarding EMU, one that is less favorable to union and the other more favorable. The unfavorable change is the strength of the dollar. EMU can be looked upon, at least partly, as a reaction against the seigniorage or money tax, which is more oppressive the weaker the dollar. The cycle of "eurofever" has risen and fallen with the weakness and strength of the dollar. Thus, with the deficits and gold conversion of the early 1960s, some early plans were made for monetary integration. These increased again the late 1960s, the Hague Summit and the Werner Plan. The breakup of the system and Europe's inability to organize a joint float dampened eurofever in the early 1970s, but U.S. inflation and depreciation in the late 1970s brought it again to the fore with the creation of the EMS. With Reaganomics and the soaring dollar, eurofever subsided. But with the weak dollar in the late 1980s, the Delors Report set the stage for EMU, all of which was accelerated by German unification and the peak of eurofever with the Maastricht treaty. A strong dollar takes away one of the most powerful arguments for EMU.

The change favorable to European economic and monetary union is the unexpected success of a few countries in moving toward the achievement of the Maastricht convergence criteria. A year ago it seemed unlikely that Italy, Spain, and Portugal would be close to the

3 percent deficit criterion. But a concerted effort by each country has brought them closer, and the markets have responded by narrowing greatly the gap between German and national interest rates.

Another factor is favorable to EMU. As you all know, budget deficits can be calculated in different ways. In its *1996 World Economic Outlook,* the IMF (relying on a study by Sheetal Chand) underscored the importance of including unfunded pension liabilities in calculating the budget deficit. The factor is particularly important in the case of such core European Union countries as Germany and France. If you allow for financing these future payments in the current deficit, the budget deficits of all countries will be higher, but the impact is very different among countries: The deficits of Germany and France, for example, are increased to a much larger extent than those of Britain and Italy. Britain could satisfy the Maastricht conditions relatively easily; its problem is that it may not want to enter. But Italy's position is no longer as inferior to that of France and Germany as the official figures show.

The same argument holds with respect to debt-to-GDP ratios. Taking into account the capitalized value of unfunded pension commitments, Britain is in a far better position than France or Germany. Italy is also in a far better relative position, taking into account the capitalized value of its unfunded pension liabilities. When or if these factors are taken into account at the Council Summit in early 1998, the position of the "Club Med" countries will be much improved relative to that of France and Germany. On these grounds, therefore, there is a better chance for the Club Med countries to go forward. If so, the Scandinavian countries may go ahead as well, as will Ireland—which makes the entry of 13 countries a distinct possibility.

Then what will Britain do? Many think Britain should stay out, but the issue remains open. I think that when Britain sees this bloc of 13 countries forming, some of its objections will be overcome, and it will see the costs of staying out as much higher. I would put the chances that Britain would enter as high as 0.5. Britain's joining would result in all EU members in EMU except Greece. And Greece's position is not as hopeless as it has been made out to be. It does have a huge budget deficit—6 to 7 percent of GDP; among EU members, it feels compelled to spend the highest proportion of its GDP on armaments. Nonetheless, Greece has the largest primary surplus, as a percent of GDP, in Europe. If Greece makes a genuine effort to put other elements of its economic house in order—which it wants to do—it could be accepted into the union as well. The huge international transfers now being made to such countries as Greece, Portugal, and Spain could be phased out more rapidly under monetary union than otherwise. Because of these considerations, I would not rule out the possibility that all 15 countries enter the EMU.

More formally, I would put the probabilities of various EMU membership scenarios as follows:

- 80 percent, that a core group including both Germany and France form a monetary union;
- 60 percent, that the union includes Germany, France, Austria, Netherlands, Belgium, Luxembourg, Denmark, Ireland, and Finland;
- 30 percent, that the above countries join and are joined by Sweden, Portugal, Spain, and Italy;
- 15 percent, that the above countries join and are joined by Britain; and
- 10 percent, that all countries, including Greece, join.

The Maastricht approach is not the only route to monetary union. Once countries have gotten control of their budget deficits, they will have the option of fixing exchange rates to the euro with very narrow margins, achieving many of the benefits of EMU without the ultimate sacrifice in monetary sovereignty. Indeed, this is the approach countries such as the Club Med countries and Greece should follow even if the European Council at its 1998 meeting rejects their application for early admittance to EMU (Mundell and Sadun, 1996). The more countries that join the bloc, the greater its chance of success. Failure to go forward would be an awesome disappointment to those who see European monetary unification as the best catalyst for a stable economic and political order on the continent.

References

Friedman, M. "Contemporary Monetary Problems, *Economic Notes,* Vol. 2, No. 1 (January-April 1973), pp. 5–18. This article reproduces a lecture given at the National Bank of Yugoslavia (March 20, 1973), published in Serbo-Croatian translation in *Jugoslovensko Bankrstvo,* No. 6 (1973), the monthly periodical of the Yugoslav Banking Association.

Mundell, R. A. "International Trade and Factor Mobility," *The American Economic Review,* XLVII, No. 3 (June 1957), pp. 321–35. Reprinted in *Readings in International Economics,* eds. R. E. Caves and H. G. Johnson (Chicago: Irwin, 1967); and Mundell (1968).

———, "Transport Costs in International Trade Theory," *The Canadian Journal of Economics and Political Science,* XXIII, No. 3 (August 1957), pp. 331–48. Reprinted in Mundell (1968).

———, "The Pure Theory of International Trade," *The American Economic Review,* L, No.1 (March 1960), pp. 68–110. Reprinted in Mundell (1968).

———, "The Monetary Dynamics of International Adjustment Under Fixed and Flexible Exchange Rates," *The Quarterly Journal of Economics,* LXXXIV, No. 2 (May 1960), pp. 227–57. Reprinted in Mundell (1968).

————, "The International Disequilibrium System," *Kyklos,* XIV, Fisc.2 (1961), pp.154–72. Reprinted in Mundell (1968).

————, "Flexible Exchange Rates and Employment Policy," *The Canadian Journal of Economics and Political Science,* XXVII, No. 4 (November 1961), pp. 509–17. Reprinted in Mundell (1968).

————, "A Theory of Optimum Currency Areas," *The American Economic Review,* LI, No. 4 (November 1961), pp. 509–17. Reprinted in Mundell (1968).

————, "The Gold Herring," U.S. Congress. Hearings on the U.S. Balance of Payments. Washington, DC: Joint Economic Committee (November 1963).

————, "Capital Mobility and Size," *The Canadian Journal of Economics and Political Science,* XXX, No. 3 (August 1964), pp. 421–31. Reprinted in Mundell (1968).

————, "The Proper Division of the Burden of International Adjustment," *The National Banking Review,* 3, No. 1 (September 1965), pp. 81–87.

————, *The International Monetary System: Conflict and Reform,* Private Planning Association of Canada (Montreal, 1965).

————, "Gold and the Gulliver Problem." Lecture presented at the University of Chicago (February 8, 1968).

————, "A Plan for a World Currency," Joint Economic Committee. Hearings Before [Reuss] Subcommittee on International Exchange and Payments (September 9, 1968).

————, "The Case for a European Currency." Paper presented at a meeting of American Management Association in New York (December 1969). Mimeo.

————, "A Plan for a European Currency." Paper presented at Optimum Currency Areas Conference in Madrid (March 1970). Reprinted in *The Economics of Common Currencies,* eds. H. Johnson and A. Swoboda (London: George Allen & Unwin Ltd., 1973), pp. 143–73.

————, "African Trade, Politics and Money." In *Africa and Monetary Integration,* ed. R. Tremblay (Montreal: Les Editions HRW, 1972), pp. 11–67. Paper originally prepared for UN Economic Commission for Africa (August 1970).

————, "The Optimum Balance of Payments Deficit and the Theory of Empires." In *Stabilization Policies in Interdependent Economies,* eds. P. Salin and E. Claassen (Amsterdam: North Holland Press, 1971), pp. 69–86.

————, "The Choice of Monetary Systems: African Currency Problems." In *Africa and Monetary Integration,* ed. R. Tremblay (Montreal: Les Editions HRW. 1972), pp. 363–68.

————, "The Geography of Inflation and the Reform of the Gold Standard." In *Geographical Aspects of Inflation Processes* (New York: American Geographical Society, 1976).

Mundell, R.A. and Arrigo Sadun. "Il *Piano di parità lira-marco:* entrare in Europa passando per Francoforte," *Rivista di Politica Economica* Anno LXXXVI-Serie III Fasciocolo VII-VIII (Luglio-Agosto, 1996), pp.121–41.

————, "The Lira-Mark Parity Plan" (with Arrigo Sadun) *Rivista di Politica Economica* (September-October 1996). English version of the above.

3

Policy Forum

Policy Forum:

Fixed Versus Floating Exchange Rates:

What's New in the Debate?

*T*HE KEY OBJECTIVES OF THE POLICY FORUM *were to flesh out new policy points in the decades long-debate on fixed versus flexible exchange rate systems and the related issue of optimum currency areas (OCA). When the OCA theory addressing the question "One money for how many?" was developed in the early 1960s by Robert A. Mundell and Ronald McKinnon, it did not focus on certain questions at the heart of the current policy debate. The policy forum sought to evaluate, under current world circumstances, the new policy-oriented developments regarding the classic debate on fixed versus floating exchange rates.*

William R. White
Bank for International Settlements

With regard to the question of whether there is anything new in the debate on fixed versus flexible exchange rates, I would say both no and yes. As to why no, allow me (since we are in Israel) to quote from the Old Testament (Ecclesiastes): "What profit a man of all his labour which he taketh under the sun? One generation passeth away and another generation cometh, but the earth abideth for ever. The thing that has been is that which shall be, and that which is done is that which shall be done, and there is no new thing under the sun."

In this spirit, I ask you to go back to the 1920s, or even before, to the debate on the pros and cons of the gold standard. Much of that debate remains very modern. As to the merits of floating, Keynes in the 1920s said that floating with domestic price stability as the goal of monetary policy would result in a more satisfactory regime than adherence to even a modified gold standard. In 1931, when Sweden was forced off the gold standard, the authorities asked a panel of prominent academics what to do. The answer again was to float with the objective of domestic price stability. I sometimes remark to my European colleagues, particularly those who worry about competitive devaluations of the sort seen in the 1930s, that there is a simple answer. The outs should be advised to adopt the framework recommended in the 1920s. If domestic price stability were the single goal of their domestic monetary policy, floating simply could not be used to engineer competitive devaluations.

As an aside about the modernity of earlier thought, there was also a strong interest in the 1920s in how market perceptions and expectations could have an important impact on the effect of policies. Keynes's contention before the Macmillan Committee—that fiscal stimulus would expand output—was met squarely by a Treasury view that the negative response in the bond market would be so great as to have the opposite effect. This is identical to the current debate about the effects of fiscal consolidation in modern Europe, albeit with the signs changed to protect the innocent!

I also suspect that the debate over fixed versus flexible rates will go on forever. I say this because Robert Mundell's 1961 paper on optimum currency areas was a reaction to the then-growing support for floating. The appeal of floating back then owed to the fact that people had lived with a fixed exchange rate regime long enough to see all its warts. More recently, of course, we have lived with floating for so long that many—particularly in Europe—have had enough time to see its warts. And so the debate will continue because the fundamental reality is that there is "no right answer."

As to what is new in the debate, the most important development has been the empirical work responding to the fact that there is "no right answer." The basic analytical framework for an optimum currency area has not changed much over the years, although Mundell continues to extend the list of reasons for joining an OCA. The enormous amount of new empirical work allows us to determine whether the size of the asymmetric shocks is large enough, the degree of labor mobility great enough, and so on, to warrant establishing a single currency area.

Also "newish" in the debate, after some twenty years of belief in efficient markets and rational expectations, is the renewed acceptance that "bubbles happen," or that bad things can occur in financial markets. I say newish because Keynes' General Theory also put a lot of emphasis on the possibility of such irrational behavior. Thus, the more efficient allocation of resources provided by financial markets also has a down side. Recognition of this down side, shifts the balance in favor of trying to fix exchange rates to avoid such speculative pressures.

The third new concept I hold Paul Masson responsible for, as he was the first to elucidate it formally. It is the distinction between reputation and credibility, or "Is John Wayne really John Wayne without his horse and rifle?" You can build reputation by doing and saying the right things, but if you have no horse or gun, you cannot deliver. A good illustration of this is the attack on some participants in the European exchange rate mechanism in 1992. At the time, the defense in some countries was simply not credible because unemployment rates were so high or banking systems so fragile that the markets knew the authorities could not credibly, and in their own self-interest, continue doing what they had to do to preserve the parity.

The fourth new thing is that the Mundell-Fleming model is increasingly seen as a special case, in which complications posed by unstable inflation expectations and debt levels are ignored in a way they cannot be ignored in the real world. These complications give rise to practical questions: for example, does fiscal restraint lower or raise the exchange rate? In the Mundell-Fleming model, which is the Washington consensus as I understand it, fiscal restraint lowers the exchange rate because a fall in the rate of interest (consequent to the restraint) causes capital outflows; hence, a depreciation. Many Europeans, on the other hand, currently argue that fiscal credibility boosts the exchange rate. Some recent research provides an analytical framework to resolve this apparent conflict. What it comes down to is that fiscal contraction lowers the risk premium required to hold a particular currency. Thus, interest rates may fall enough, "crowding in" investment and other things, so that a depreciation is not required to restore equilibrium at full employment. In addition, take the case of a country with a large external deficit that has to be serviced and that is denominated in its own currency; for example, the United States today. If domestic interest rates fell far enough, the result might be an external benefit large enough to preclude the need to devalue the exchange rate to preserve a sustainable current account deficit over time.

The fifth new point attracting considerable attention in Europe is the adequacy of market discipline to force sustainable or prudent fiscal policies. Many argue that market discipline will suffice, while others disagree. Some Europeans, in their proposed stability pact, have weighed in on the side of the skeptics, as the pact effectively assumes that markets are insufficient in and of themselves to ensure stability.

My last point about new developments is that the debate about fixed versus flexible exchange rates is now being engaged in emerging market countries, in the context of domestic financial deregulation and increasing international capital mobility, in a way none of us would have thought possible twenty years ago. Moreover, the analytical framework being used to help guide the selection of an exchange rate regime in emerging countries is generally the same framework being used in industrial economies. Having said that, the starting point for many of these emerging market economies is quite different. They have a more volatile macroeconomic environment, transitional problems associated with weaker banking systems, weak financial infrastructures, and a lack of security markets. All of these complications are germane to their choice of exchange rate regime at this time, recognizing again that there is "no right answer"! However, the underlying analytic tools are the same and, with time, the practical circumstances that distinguish emerging from industrial economies will become less important.

Jacob A. Frenkel
Bank of Israel

The debate is not about fixed versus flexible exchange rates, it is about good and bad policies. As Mundell wrote, there is a "good fix" and a "bad fix," a "good flex" and a "bad flex." Therefore, the real issue is which policy regime will be conducive to better policies. In this regard, I agree with Bill White that it depends on the circumstances.

On the optimum currency area, I quote John Stuart Mill: "So much barbarism, however, still remains in the transactions of the most civilized nations that almost all independent countries choose to assert their nationality by having, to their own inconvenience and that of their neighbors, a peculiar currency of their own." Mill adds that: "The progress of political improvement" will bring about the disappearance of this "barbarism." Was he right? Will barbarism disappear with the introduction of the euro, at least in one part of the world? Is it "barbarism" for nations to have their own currency?

The debate about fixed versus flexible exchange rates will continue, as it will about good versus bad policies. One of the reasons is because we are not working in a laboratory and the subject of the analysis is society, which operates with memories. Thus, once you have implemented a set of policies at a given point in time and you try to repeat those policies, you might get different results since individuals with memories and experience may respond differently.

But we now have a new reality: one in which monetary policy is recognized to operate with lags, and thus we have a theory requiring a medium-term perspective and no fine-tuning. We have a framework within which monetary authorities are granted independence to implement that approach. Similarly, fiscal policy is known to be inflexible; it is a rigid policy instrument, both on the spending and the tax sides. And finally, commercial (or trade) policy is passé, at least legally so, which is why the General Agreement on Tariffs and Trade (GATT) gave way to the World Trade Organization.

Therefore, what macroeconomic policy instruments remain? With monetary policy conducted with a medium-term perspective by an independent central bank, fiscal policy also having a medium-term perspective with no fine tuning, and commercial policy being illegal, all that remains is, possibly, policy coordination. But the Germans say to "cooperate" rather than coordinate. But cooperate on what? The IMF has come up with the best response in its efforts to facilitate an improved economic data base on the part of its member countries—thereby helping to set transparent "rules of the game." Bill White has identified the right approach for cooperation; it lies in the area of supervision, timely provision of information, and capital requirements for banks. These are the areas in which one needs to set the transparent game rules.

Thus, globalization and clear and transparent rules of the game have entered as fine-tuning the policy mix in the short term exited. And why? Because capital markets are quick and have memory and because the future—through the processes of expectations and capitalization—is converted quickly into the present. When we speak about the global network, we speak about it in the context of trade, capital, and information. And the rules of the game are therefore rules that ensure consistency rather than operational policy actions.

The world today is multi-polar, not only in terms of the center of gravity among which exchange rates can be set, but also in terms of different concepts of poles. A geographical pole is linked to trade; functional poles are linked by level of economic advancement (for example, developing, industrial, and transitional economies); and political poles—economies previously communists, capitalists, or centrally planned—are linked in many respects. The exchange rate is just one mechanism creating a connection in this multitude of roles.

To sum up, in the modern world with huge capital markets that respond rapidly to policies, no exchange rate system can protect against bad policies. And there are not enough reserves in the world to help a country peg systematically the wrong exchange rate.

Israel's Experience

In Israel, there is practically no exchange rate regime or system we have not tried. These experiments, however, have had a logic to them. In seeking to break hyperinflation, we had to break from the past. We needed a nominal anchor, such as the fixed exchange rate introduced in the mid 1980s. But this could not be a long-term proposition as long as domestic inflation differed significantly from inflation abroad. So first we made discrete adjustments to the periodically fixed exchange rate; then we let the rate fluctuate within a narrow band; later we widened the band; and, finally, we moved to a crawling band. In the process, we sought to reconcile two features: some anchoring properties from the exchange rate regime, and some consistency properties between the nominal aspects of the regime, the price framework, and the exchange rate framework.

This is why we have gravitated to the current system of the crawling band. We have learned several lessons in the process, the key one being the continuing need to allocate responsibility between policy targets and policy instruments. We recognize the widespread experience in many countries in the world, according to which monetary policy has a comparative advantage in dealing with nominal magnitudes, especially with prices. Therefore, it stands to reason that this will be the appropriate market classification, or division of responsibilities. Thus, in the conduct of monetary policy, we pay special attention to meeting the government's inflation target.

We felt it was important for the government to cast the target within the broader framework of macroeconomic management. The real test, however, is when a dilemma arises. If inflation accelerates and exceeds the target, interest rates must be raised. But if the higher interest rate induces capital inflows, the currency appreciates and poses a problem. In Israel, the industrialists are finding themselves in the unique position of (implicitly) favoring inflation. They would like, of course, to have price stability so their costs do not rise. But because interest rates in Israel have been geared to reducing inflation, and because we had to raise interest rates in pursuit of the inflation target—and the higher interest rates had caused an appreciation seen as costly to the business sector—businesses were willing to tolerate a higher inflation target. This would allow for a lower interest rate, which would permit the currency to depreciate in nominal terms and help us all (at least temporarily) live "happily ever after."

But we will not live happily ever after because after a relatively short period of time, inflation will accelerate and, as a result, the real exchange rate will not be affected. In the old days, economists did not give due attention to the distinction between the nominal and real exchange rate. When you speak about a crawling band and division of responsibility between the monetary and other authorities, you must first be sure you have the instrument to bring about lower inflation so you can control interest rates. But then, as capital flows in, the currency appreciates. You must then make sure your economy can sustain at least a partial appreciation. And once you reach the limit of what you believe the economy can sustain, you must intervene, and at the same time sterilize the monetary consequences of the intervention. But Mundell taught that sterilization is not viable over the long run. The key policy issue is to assess what the long run is. And therefore you need enough reserves to sterilize, with the hope that the fiscal side will be "in line" to ensure that the real exchange rate does not begin to appreciate as you are trying to disinflate. In advising countries to adopt a crawling band, or inflation targets, one must have a high expectation that fiscal policy will generally being in line. If it is not, if there is a large budget deficit, pressures from the real economy will arise for real appreciation, with considerable pressure to respond with monetary expansion—which will just generate inflation. Thus, I urge that policy makers are first sure they have fiscal discipline.

This brings me back to my opening remark. The debate is not about fixed versus flexible exchange rate, but about good versus bad policies. In terms of policy regimes, it is about which regime is conducive for the good fix, the bad fix, the good flex, and the bad flex. The answer is not universal, as it must reflect the particular circumstances.

Richard Portes
London Business School and Centre for Economic Policy Research

The world has given us a new laboratory as economists in Eastern Europe—specifically, with respect to choosing an exchange rate, macroeconomic stabilization, and dealing with capital inflows. We have already learned useful lessons in this laboratory. The first lesson concerns the choice of nominal anchor in stabilization. The issues presented themselves in particular ways in Central and Eastern Europe, by countries on the road toward accession to the European Union. With respect to using a monetary aggregate as a nominal anchor, the argument was that this was impossible since institutions were changing too fast. In fact, the data show that velocity has actually been relatively stable in these countries, and that one can arrive at reasonably stable demand functions for money. Nonetheless, it is hard to forecast inflation and the growth of output, and, hence, hard to formulate a target for a monetary aggregate. This is the problem with money-based stabilization.

Inflation targeting is the fashion of the moment in many of our countries. Eastern Europe, however, is characterized by underdeveloped financial markets, inefficient transmission mechanisms, fiscal problems, problems in using interest rates against inflation, doubtful central bank independence, and so forth. Thus, in practice, these countries have not chosen inflation targets.

On the other hand, nominal exchange rate policy, or exchange-rate-based stabilization, has been used. But this requires a reasonable level of reserves, and possibly some backing from the international organizations—the IMF in particular—as well as a prior or contemporaneous fiscal stabilization. In fact, most of those countries that could have used exchange-rate-based stabilization have done so. Others have had to use monetary targeting.

The results are interesting. As I have just suggested, there is a selection bias—that is, the countries better placed are the ones able to use exchange-rate-based stabilization. You might think that the outcome would therefore favor exchange-rate-based stabilization. But the data do not back this up. Monetary targets perform better than you might expect in Albania, Croatia, Slovenia, Latvia, and Lithuania—which did not adopt their exchange rate and peg their currency until after stabilization had been well launched.

The exchange-rate-based stabilizations do yield favorable results on the nominal variables. In Poland, the Czech Republic, Estonia, Slovakia, and Hungary, the nominal variables look good. Output on the other hand, looks terrible. Why don't we see the Bruno-Easterly effect (1996) observed in so many countries and in so many instances of stabilization—that is, output rising in an exchange-rate-based stabilization, rather than the tremendous depression we saw in Eastern Europe? Was something wrong with the stabilization programs or ill-adapted to the circumstances of these economies? I think there were important errors, but the point here is that that regime did reduce inflation very widely, and in a number of countries, very successfully.

Post stabilization, one cannot hold the peg as real appreciation goes too far. There is some degree of inertial inflation, as illustrated in Poland. That is one problem. Second, a country can receive massive capital inflows even if it does not have that inertial inflation, as in the Czech Republic, and these can force a country off the peg. Hence, we are seeing a crawling peg in Poland, and a frequent backward-looking adjustment of the peg in Hungary—and then, from mid–1995, a pre-announced crawl; while the Czech Republic has adopted bands, moving from a single parity with no band, to a 7½ percent band at the same parity. Part of this is due to the capital inflow problem. While such capital inflows are a boon, they pose difficult challenges for policy makers.

This has already manifested itself in a wide range of countries in Eastern Europe. The Czech Republic and Poland, in particular, but also Estonia, Albania, Slovenia, Croatia, and Slovakia have all had significant capital inflows and have had to deal with the macroeconomic consequences. During 1994–96, net capital inflows into these countries were on the order of 6–7 percent of GDP—a magnitude that exceeded

...

that of the major Latin American cases. Confidence increased in these countries with fiscal consolidation, real interest rates became significantly positive. It became clear that a real exchange rate appreciation would occur over the medium term, and macroeconomic expansion finally began.

How to cope with heavy capital inflows? Some of the inflows are associated with a natural and sustainable current account deficit, with which one should not interfere. If the problem were mainly excess demand, the answer might simply be to raise interest rates and let that choke off excess demand, and the capital inflow associated with the expansion. But that just spurs more capital inflows, and the Spanish experience of the late 1980s best illustrates this. It tends also to make the exchange rate appreciate further.

So what to do? If you wish to maintain the peg, you try to sterilize the capital inflows. But the evidence from Eastern Europe and elsewhere suggests that this is a trap, especially in the context of major sustained inflows. Sterilization can actually end up raising interest rates and stimulating more inflows. What it certainly does is to generate a heavy quasi-fiscal burden in the interest rate differential a country ends up paying to pursue that policy over any length of time.

Unsterilized intervention just results in the real exchange rate appreciation you may have been trying to avoid, but through inflation rather than the nominal exchange rate move. Therefore, the right solution is probably to let the peg go in order to allow the real appreciation that is bound to come through nominal appreciation. That is easier to reverse with floating—if the capital flows themselves reverse—rather than trying to reverse the inflation you get otherwise.

The bottom line is that the choice is not between fixed or floating. It is a choice between trying to prevent real appreciation—pressure on the tradeable sector and the development of a large current account deficit—and letting it happen either through a float or inflation. Which choice you opt for depends on whether you believe the inflows will persist. If you believe they will, you must accommodate them. The trouble is that you do not know, which is about as far as we have progressed to date. The experiments continue, and we shall see what happens.

With respect to the exchange rate regime in the medium run, the transition countries must allow nominal appreciation, which will yield on trend a real appreciation. This is what transition is about—achieving a rapid productivity increase, one substantially faster than in one's trading partners. And the right way to achieve it in this context is probably through crawling bands, which should not be too narrow. The country may want to reduce the crawl rate and the band width over time, depending on how far stabilization goes. In this connection, I would not put as much priority as the IMF is currently doing on trying to reduce the rate of inflation still further in these countries.

Turning to European Union issues, even countries with a fixed rate may want to switch to a more flexible regime as they move toward accession. Accession will mean greater integration of their domestic international markets with the overall European Union financial market, and therefore more volatile short run capital flows. What about the Maastricht criteria? They are irrelevant in the context of accession, and that is recognized certainly in the European Commission, although not by East European politicians. The Maastricht criteria are only relevant to countries that want to join the euro. Even if some of these countries were to accede to the European Union in 2002, it is highly unlikely they would go immediately into the euro.

The relevant Copenhagen criterion for membership is acceptance of the obligations of economic and monetary union. This means that if they are outs—as they would be for some time with respect to the single currency—they would still have to participate in whatever exchange rate mechanism is finally settled on between the ins and the outs. This creates a potential problem of exchange rate policy. The danger is surely not competitive devaluation. Indeed, these countries are going to experience real appreciation. But the European Union may try to force upon them a degree of nominal exchange rate stability for which they are unprepared. It would not be the first time that Franco-German rigidity might prevail in European Union affairs.

Manuel Guitián
International Monetary Fund

Bill White cited Keynes' comment that floating, with price stability as the goal of monetary policy, would constitute a perfectly reasonable international regime. But in his *A Treatise on Money,* Keynes also wrote of methods of supernational currency management, describing as "the maximum" among possible regimes, the establishment of "a Supernational Bank to which the Central Banks of the world would stand in much the same relation as their own member banks stand to them." Thus, over a half a century ago, Keynes outlined an arrangement that presaged efforts such as those now rapidly approaching completion for a European central bank. It is clear, then, that Keynes took all sides of an argument, and very persuasively at that. In my mind, he was able to do this by concentrating on the dilemmas that arise in the search for balance between national and international interests.

When a decision must be made on the adoption of an exchange rate regime, as Jacob Frenkel has stressed, the focus must be placed where it belongs, that is, on whether the regime will foster good or bad economic policies. From this standpoint, what the concept of currency areas added to the debate of fixed versus floating exchange rates is the idea that an optimum currency domain has really little to do with national frontiers. In his seminal article on the subject, Mundell explored the question of whether all national currencies should float. In other words, whether nations should take it for granted that flexible exchange rates represented an appropriate regime for each and all of them.

Experience on this front seems to conform to a cyclical pattern: countries adopt a fixed exchange rate regime; they become disenchanted with the constraints they impose on their national policy autonomy and they move toward flexible exchange rate arrangements; they then balk at the uncertainties created by unfettered national policy discretion and seek to contain them by reverting toward less flexible arrangements.

The advantages of fixed exchange rate regimes are of course those of "pooling." Countries with inappropriate economic policies "export" part of their imbalances, making others share in their costs. Discomfort with such exports grows over time, particularly in those countries with relatively better economic policies—those that "import" the costs of imbalance and export the benefits of balance—and pressure builds up for insulation and, hence, for floating. In this manner, international exchange arrangements tend to move from rules to discretion, reflecting shifts in the balance of national and international interests, to which I referred earlier.

The problem with discretion-based international regimes, of course, is that they make it harder to assign unambiguously responsibilities for policy adjustments. In situations of imbalance, should primary responsibility for policy correction fall upon deficit or surplus countries? The practical counterpart of this assignment dilemma is to identify the inappropriateness of policies and the consequent need for weighing a variety of policy indicators, not all of which point in the same direction or are of the same importance. In this context, the merits of the simplicity of a fixed exchange rate are clear: domestic policies should be compatible with the external constraint or be appropriately adjusted. It is, in essence, a single indicator system.

In a nutshell, then, a fixed exchange rate exposes countries to external shocks while a flexible rate insulates them from such shocks. But let us examine this observation in the context of developments in the world economy over the last fifty years. During this period, all countries decided—and broadly succeeded in the endeavor—to open their economies to international trade in goods and services, that is, the current account of their balance of payments. Thus, a progressive move toward integration of national markets for goods and services has been under way for long. Inevitably, with it came a growing liberalization of capital account transactions, a process in which countries have gone well beyond the commitments they undertook after World War II. As you may know, this issue is under active discussion now among the IMF membership, as it concerns the possible amendment of the Articles of Agreement, which still contemplate the use of capital controls.

Accordingly, the issues of exchange regimes and their relationship with policy appropriateness have to be seen from the perspective of a closely integrated economic setting. This is important in the context of the debate on currency areas, since one aspect of the debate typically focuses on the loss of policy autonomy entailed by participating in a common currency arrangement. Conceptually, this limitation is well established, of course. Possibly more relevant, though, is that in today's world environment, even without common currency areas, all countries have lost an important measure of policy autonomy because of the growing integration of national economies internationally. This is the case even under flexible exchange arrangements. Thus, neither fixed exchange rates in themselves entail as much autonomy loss as typically thought, nor do flexible exchange rates ensure as much insulation as generally believed. Country policies at present are all subject to the discipline of market forces, which impose a far sterner constraint than any institutional arrangement.

The evolution of the concept of currency areas offers some interesting perspectives. In his original article Mundell stressed the importance of factor mobility—in particular, labor mobility—in a setting of downwardly rigid wages and prices. Subsequently, other features were identified, including the degree of openness of the economy, its product differentiation, financial integration, and the nature of the shocks to which it is typically exposed. Later on, particularly in Europe, the discussion shifted from the structural characteristics of an economy to a different set of criteria for determining the suitability of participation in a common currency area. These criteria included: whether countries have similar inflation targets and prospects; whether other economic policy objectives are shared; and whether countries have the same attitude to fiscal and, more generally, macroeconomic discipline. Questions such as these are behind the emphasis of the Maastricht treaty on macroeconomic policy convergence. It would be, of course, unfortunate, if such emphasis on the macroeconomic policy side were to divert attention from critical microeconomic requirements, such as achieving factor mobility and factor price flexibility. Not only are these essential to confront

Europe's current unemployment problems, they are also prerequisites for the efficient functioning of the European monetary system.

Mundell's seminal idea on optimum currency areas led initially to a flurry of research followed by a relatively long period of silence, other than the continuing interest in Europe in the context of monetary unification efforts. When Mundell wrote his original article, the European Common Market, then recently established, consisted of just six countries, and not much thought was given to monetary union. Since then, though, the European Union has expanded and become closely integrated; some of its members exhibit some of the characteristics of a common currency area. But among those characteristics, the original Mundellian one of labor mobility and flexibility is yet to be attained, which makes it the one deserving most attention.

In sum, much has happened in the international economy since currency areas were introduced by Mundell. Europe is moving fast in that direction, but so is the world economy, albeit at a slower pace. I am not predicting that we will have a world central bank any time soon. But the scope for insulating a national economy through exchange rate flexibility is vanishing rapidly. With capital mobility, it looked as if only a polar choice existed between exchange regimes: float or join a common currency area. But perfectly mobile capital tends to erode the insulating powers of floating rates. With integration, the world is now much closer to a currency area than it was thirty-five years ago. For a currency area's efficient operation, it will be necessary to ensure that microeconomic conditions are, and remain, appropriate. And countries seeking to join a monetary union confront the challenge of generating domestic cost and price flexibility to compensate for the absence of exchange rate flexibility as a possible instrument of adjustment.

Assaf Razin
Tel Aviv University

In closing this policy forum, I would like to address one aspect of EMU, which is a deflation bias that may be caused by a European central bank's high degree of independence with an exclusive inflation goal. The EMU is similar in some ways to the resumption of the gold standard in the United States in 1897. The gold standard was pre-announced, very much like Maastricht, and it eventually materialized—which is also likely with EMU. But it was then followed by price deflation and low growth, and only the discovery of gold mines at the end of the nineteenth century provided some growth relief.

Conference participants have cited various reasons why the euro should be stronger than the deutsche mark or why the ECB should be expected to be more conservative. I would like to mention three: First, the board of governors, including the governor, of the EMU will have no direct accountability to any particular national body, making it freer to achieve its target, which will be almost exclusively an inflation target. Second, initially, the ECB will try to build its reputation as an anti-inflation institution, which will make it even tougher. And third, the ECB will be more independent than the Bundesbank, since the Bundesbank's regulatory role will remain with national authorities and not with the ECB. Hence, monetary policy will not take account of the effect on the balance sheets of banks, which will be less of a hurdle for conducting conservative monetary policy.

My two colleagues at the IMF, Tom Krueger and Doug Laxton (see Krueger and others in this volume), and I looked at, among other things, the quantitative effects of low employment scenarios. In so doing, we have used the IMF model, the acronym for the Mundell-Fleming model, incorporating rational expectations discovered later on. Our analysis suggests the possibility of large quantitative output losses in the next three to five years, with not much gain in terms of inflation. And those countries either temporarily or permanently out of the arrangement will fare better, at least during the transition.

A separate issue is how to cope with heavy capital flows during disinflation periods. This is the issue raised by Jacob Frenkel in the context of Israel's recent experience. A common feature of some of the recent disinflation episodes is that those countries that used capital controls suffered relatively small output losses. Capital controls improve the so-called sacrifice ratio (the percentage rise in unemployment for a 1 percent decline in inflation) since they limit the adverse effects of real exchange rate fluctuations caused by free capital flows on aggregate demand. Thus, the Tobin tax on capital inflows is advisable in periods of disinflation.

References

Bruno, M. and W. Easterly, "Inflation's Children: Tales of Crises," *American Economic Review* (May 1996).

4

New Developments

The Endogeneity of the Optimum Currency Area Criteria

Jeffrey A. Frankel and Andrew K. Rose

EVERYONE STUDYING EUROPEAN ECONOMIC and monetary union (EMU) cites the theory of optimum currency areas (OCA): whether a country should join the currency union depends on such parameters as the extent of trade with other European Union members and the correlation of the country's income with that of other members. Few economists have focused on one of the most interesting aspects of this issue: that trade patterns and income correlations are endogenous. A country could fail the OCA criteria for membership today, and yet, if it goes ahead and joins anyway, could, as the result of joining, satisfy the OCA criteria in the future.

The few economists who have identified the importance of the endogeneity of trade patterns and income correlation are divided on the nature of the relationship between the two. This is an important empirical question, which may hold the key to the answer regarding whether it is in a country's interest to join EMU.

We review the OCA theory, highlighting the role of trade links and income links. We then discuss and analyze the endogeneity of these parameters. From a theoretical viewpoint, the effect of increased trade integration on the cross-country correlation of business cycle activity is ambiguous. Reduced trade barriers can result in increased industrial specialization by country and therefore more asynchronous business cycles resulting from industry-specific shocks. On the other hand, increased integration may result in more highly correlated business cycles because of demand shocks or intra-industry trade. Happily, this ambiguity is theoretical rather than empirical.

We present econometric evidence suggesting strongly that as trade links between countries strengthen, their national incomes become more highly correlated (rather than less correlated, as some claim). Using a panel of 30 years of data from 20 industrial countries, we find a strong positive relationship between the degree of bilateral trade intensity and the cross-country bilateral correlation of business cycle activity; that is, greater integration historically has resulted in more highly synchronized cycles.

This has important implications for the OCA criteria. It means that a naive examination of historical data gives a biased picture of the effects of EMU entry on a country. Some countries may appear, on the basis of historical data, to be poor candidates for EMU entry. But EMU entry per se, for whatever reason, may provide a substantial impetus for trade expansion; this in turn may result in more highly correlated business cycles. That is, a country is more likely to satisfy the criteria for entry into a currency union ex post than ex ante.

Openness and the Cost of Fixing Exchange Rates in a Mundell-Fleming World

Daniel Gros and Alfred Steinherr

THE THEORY OF OPTIMUM CURRENCY AREAS (OCA) pioneered by Robert Mundell in 1961 has become fashionable again. European economic and monetary union (EMU) is surely the main cause of the new wave of OCA literature in recent years. One basic idea that seems to be widely accepted is that a smaller European Union member country should have a stronger interest in participating in EMU because it is more open. This presumption is based on two elements: that the larger the degree of openness, the higher the gain from EMU from reduced transaction costs; and that the larger the degree of openness, the lower the cost of abandoning the nominal exchange rate as an economic policy instrument. We do not address the first element; our paper concentrates exclusively on factors that determine the costs and show that the widely accepted presumption that they diminish with openness is wrong.

We use a tool developed by Mundell to address a question he first raised: What does the Mundell-Fleming model imply for the choice of fixed versus flexible exchange rates? As it is not possible to re-examine this fundamental issue in all its aspects, we concentrate on one element of the question that has received little attention in the literature, namely, does the cost of losing the exchange rate adjustment instrument increase with the degree of openness? This issue has received little attention because the answer seemed to be obvious: of course, a higher degree of openness reduces the cost of fixing exchange rates!

McKinnon (1963) established the presumption that the costs of joining a monetary union decline with the degree of openness. In international economics textbooks and surveys on the theory of OCA, a negative relationship between the degree of openness and the costs of joining a monetary union is usually presented as almost obvious. Krugman (1990) and De Grauwe (1994) are two popular examples. It is somewhat surprising that most of the literature on monetary integration, and especially that on EMU, has accepted this standard point of view. The basic ideas leading to this "perceived wisdom" are difficult to pinpoint because those who accept it apparently believe it does not need the support of precise arguments. The main argument in Krugman (1990) is that it is easier to correct a trade deficit of, for example, 1 percent of GDP if trade accounts for 20 percent of GDP than if trade accounts for 5 percent of GDP. This might be true, but a more open country is also more likely to run large trade imbalances than a less open one.

The presumption in the literature is difficult to comprehend if one poses the question in more general terms: In the presence of nominal rigidities, the nominal exchange rate is the only adjustment instrument that impinges directly on the tradable sector of the economy. If this sector becomes more important, will this adjustment instrument become more or less important? Put this way, the presumption should go the other way.

Any statement about the cost of fixing exchange rates must obviously be based on an assumption concerning the alternative. We compare fixed exchange rates with two alternatives to make the results more robust. One alternative is to let the exchange rate float but use monetary policy to stabilize income. This use of monetary policy implies that the exchange rate is implicitly also an (intermediate) policy target. Another alternative is to let the exchange rate float freely and keep the money supply constant. This might not be the best alternative if one takes into account that the costs will always be measured in terms of the stabilization of income. But it provides a natural benchmark given that it may not be feasible to stabilize income if a number of different intertwining shocks affect the economy at the same time.

Findings

We retain two key insights: First, the cost of fixing exchange rates increases with openness if one considers external shocks. This is intuitively plausible. Having the "wrong" exchange rates hurts more when trade is important than if the economy is closed. Second, for domestic real shocks, a higher degree of openness diminishes the impact of a given shock on domestic demand and output. Hence, the cost of fixing the exchange rate diminishes if the main source of shocks is domestic. This is true, however, only from the point of view of the country concerned. If one were to take into account the interests of the rest of the world as well, the conclusion might well be different. We were not able to follow this line of thought since it requires a two-country model. This difficulty does not apply to the case of external shocks, such as the one considered by Mundell in his seminar paper on OCA, namely, shocks that shift demand from one country to another. We therefore concentrate on the case of external shocks.

One practical conclusion of our result is that if one wants to estimate the importance of the exchange rate as an adjustment instrument, one should not look only at the degree of openness, but at a combination of the degree of openness and a measure of the importance of external shocks. A very open economy with an export structure differing considerably from the European Union average (Finland?) would lose much more from no longer having the exchange rate as an adjustment instrument than a country that also has a different export structure but is less open.

Our paper does not pretend to lead to a clear criterion on whether or not a country should join EMU. The brief discussion of the *net* costs/benefits of fixing the exchange rate indicates that openness could either be irrelevant or enhance the balance between costs and benefits, whether it be positive or negative. Hence, it should no longer be accepted uncritically that net costs are strictly decreasing with openness as is usually assumed.

References

Adrian, T. and D. Gros, "The Degree of Openness and the cost of Fixing Exchange Rates," CEPS, manuscript (Brussels, 1996).

De Grauwe, P., *The Economics of Monetary Integration* (Oxford University Press, 1994).

Krugman, P., "Policy Problems of a Monetary Union," in De Grauwe, P. and L. Papademos, "The European Monetary System in the 1990s" (CEPS, Brussels, and Bank of Greece, 1990), pp. 48–64.

McKinnon, R. L., "Optimum Currency Areas," *American Economic Review,* 53 (1963), pp. 717–25.

Exchange Market Pressure and Exchange Rate Management: Perspectives from the Theory of Optimum Currency Areas

Tamim Bayoumi and Barry Eichengreen

OBERT MUNDELL IS RIGHTLY REGARDED as the father of the theory of optimum currency areas. The theory he originated, while never lacking in patrimony, was for many years orphaned by the economics profession. In looking at the number of articles with "optimum currency area" in the title over time, one sees that only in recent years, with impetus from the debate over European monetary unification, has scholarship on this subject taken off.

Along with its time profile, a conspicuous feature of optimum currency area (OCA) literature is the paucity of empirical analysis. Until recently, most of the major contributions were theoretical. To the extent that empirical work on exchange rate behavior and the choice of exchange rate regime acknowledged the predictions of OCA theory, it adopted a skeptical tone. The following conclusion by Charles Goodhart aptly summarizes the consensus view.

> "The evidence therefore suggests that the theory of optimum currency areas has relatively little predictive power. Virtually all independent sovereign states have separate currencies, and changes in sovereign states lead rapidly to accompanying adjustments in monetary autonomy. The boundaries of states rarely coincide exactly with optimum currency areas, and changes in boundaries causing changes in currency domains rarely reflect shifts in optimum currency areas."

We suggest that this conclusion—specifically, the portion represented by the first sentence in the passage above—is premature. Factors pointed to by OCA theory actually go a long way toward explaining the variability of exchange rates across countries. Goodhart may be right that the boundaries of political jurisdictions and currency areas almost always coincide, but the behavior of the exchange rates linking the monies of these separate sovereign jurisdictions are in good part explicable in OCA terms.

This will not surprise careful readers of Mundell's article, which was in fact written with the exchange rates between national currencies in mind. Mundell sought not to reorganize the world's monetary geography along OCA lines but to demonstrate that the case for stabilizing the exchange rates between national currencies was analytically no weaker than the case for denying regions within countries their own currencies (a policy that governments demonstrably preferred). His particular conclusion was that the regions of the United States—and, for their part, the regions of Canada—no better approximated an optimum currency area than the two countries together. Given that the United States and Canada chose to fix (by eliminating) the exchange rates between their regions, they should not hesitate to peg the exchange rate between their national currencies.

Our analysis begins by demonstrating that the factors underscored by the OCA theory explain much of the observed variability of exchange rates across countries. We then document that these correlations are plausibly interpreted in terms of OCA theory. That theory suggests that governments, in choosing an exchange rate policy, will want to balance the benefits of exchange rate variability—which will be greatest where asymmetric shocks are large and there is the most need for relative price adjustments—against the costs—which will be greatest in relatively small, relatively open economies where the transactions value of the currency deteriorates the most with exchange rate variability. Asymmetric shocks will increase the pressure for the exchange rate to change; small size and trade dependence will increase the pressure for intervention to limit its fluctuation. We construct separate measures of exchange market pressure and exchange market intervention to verify that asymmetric shocks affect mainly the intensity of exchange market pressure, while country size and openness affect mainly the magnitude of intervention.

We find that variables from the OCA theory—principally, proxies for asymmetric shocks—go a long way toward explaining variations across countries in the intensity of exchange market pressure. The explanatory power of OCA theory is not complete: in addition to variables measuring asymmetric disturbances, our measure of exchange market pressure depends on financial market variables, in particular, the incidence of controls on capital account transactions and the depth of domestic financial markets, as well as the structure of the international monetary system in which a particular bilateral exchange rate is embedded.

Nonetheless, this analysis again suggests that OCA variables have significant explanatory power as to the degree of underlying exchange rate pressures. We also find that the variables suggested by OCA theory have considerable explanatory power for patterns of intervention (again, along with the overall structure of the world monetary system). However, which exchange market pressures mainly depend upon measures of the cost of an OCA (basically, variables measuring the extent of asymmetric shocks), intervention is largely correlated with measures of the benefits from a stable currency, measured in our work by country size and the extent of bilateral trade links.

Our overall conclusion is thus that variables pointed to by OCA theory appear to affect the behavior of bilateral exchange rates through both market conditions and official intervention. But the two sets of considerations pointed to by the OCA literature, which balances the costs of an exchange rate peg in the presence of asymmetric shocks against the enhanced transactions value of money when the exchange rate is stabilized, operate through different channels: asymmetric shocks are the main source of exchange market pressure, while proxies for the deterioration in the transactions value of money owing to floating provide the main motivation for intervention. This provides a useful dichotomy for thinking about the evolution of the international monetary system.

These overall results are clear-cut and intuitively plausible. Asymmetric shocks translate into exchange rate variability mainly by creating exchange market pressure, while the loss in transactions services associated with exchange rate variability (which we proxy by country size) and the intensity of trade links affect the exchange rate mainly through the incentive to intervene. In short, OCA costs result in exchange rate pressures, and OCA benefits in intervention.

These conclusions also have broader implications for how we think about countries' choice of exchange rate regime. One view is that the world is divided into natural monetary groupings, which are functions of countries' economic structures, and that researchers should devote their energies to identifying these structural determinants. Another view is that exchange rate arrangements reflect instead the policy choices of governments acting in their self interest; thus, researchers should try to explain why governments attach greater or lesser weight to exchange rate stability and how that weight is a function of political circumstances. Our results, perhaps not surprisingly, lead us to conclude that the answer is not one or the other, but that both sets of factors influence observed exchange rate behavior.

One extension of this analysis is to developing countries. Much of the literature on choice of exchange rate regime relates to the developing countries. It would be interesting therefore to explore the extent to which our conclusions carry over to a larger, more heterogeneous sample of countries. A second extension is to the debate over European monetary unification. One could use equations such as those estimated above to forecast out of sample. Econometric estimates such as those in our paper could be used in conjunction with forecasts of the independent variables to predict which European countries will possess OCA characteristics in the future—that is, which ones will have characteristics consistent with maintaining a stable exchange rate. In our preliminary work on this topic, this approach identifies as prime candidates for European economic and monetary union the same countries on which the markets are currently betting (as judged by the convergence of bond yields): Germany, the Benelux countries, Austria, and Ireland. We take this as further confirmation that the theory of optimum currency areas has considerable explanatory power.

EMU: Ins, Outs, and the Macroeconomic Effects Of Alternative Monetary Policy Rules*

Thomas Krueger, Douglas Laxton, and Assaf Razin

OST OF THE INDUSTRIAL COUNTRIES of Western Europe are politically committed to strive toward a monetary union with the
circulation of a common currency set to begin early in the
next century. The resulting replacement of national monies, and national
monetary policies, is likely to have profound economic implications.
The implications depend to some extent on the countries participating
and may be different for the ins and outs of monetary union. As it stands,
not all European Union countries are likely to participate in stage 3 of
European economic and monetary union (EMU) from the outset. Some
have already opted not to participate as part of the first group (Denmark
and the United Kingdom), while others may be unable to meet the
Maastricht criteria in time and may be ruled ineligible to participate from
the beginning.

The countries joining EMU will experience a change in the decision
making process and focus of their monetary policy. In stage 3, the decisions over monetary policy will be made by the European central bank
(ECB) and the system of the national central banks. While some of the
key policy aspects remain to be decided (EMI, 1997), monetary policy
will be applied uniformly across EMU members. Of course, there is already a relatively uniform monetary policy across participants in the exchange rate mechanism (ERM) as most central banks are oriented toward
maintaining exchange rate stability vis-à-vis other participants. This has
effectively resulted in most countries following a policy that is con-

* We thank Susanna Mursula for excellent research assistance. The views expressed are
those of the authors and do not necessarily represent those of the IMF.

strained by the conduct of the Bundesbank. With already one central bank as the "leader"—severely limiting the scope for independent monetary policy of others—the question arises whether the conduct of monetary policy would be very different under EMU than under the current ERM system.

A fundamental difference from the current system can be expected to arise under EMU because of the participatory role for each member in the ECB. Under the current system, the Bundesbank has stressed consistently that it is guided by domestic economic developments and prospects (primarily, its mandate with respect to price stability of the German mark). By contrast, even if the ECB were pursuing its mandate with similar vigor, its focus would be on price stability for the euro—that is, on inflation for a group of countries and not just Germany. And to the extent that the countries participating in EMU are subject to country-specific shocks, or their cyclical positions are not fully synchronized, the conduct of monetary policy is likely to differ under EMU from the current Bundesbank-dominated context.

This new conduct of the ECB can potentially offer gains for non-German participants in EMU as monetary policy of the ECB can be expected to take into account some of the country-specific shocks in their economies, especially if these are severe enough to have significant economic consequences region-wide. For example, a substantial negative demand shock in a country like France could be expected to result in some monetary easing in the euro region, if the ECB were to follow a policy regime similar to that currently pursued by the Bundesbank, but with a focus on economic developments (notably inflation) for the euro region as a whole (Krueger, Laxton, and Razin, 1997).

While the ECB can be expected to take economic developments in the whole euro region into account, how will it actually conduct its monetary policy, and to what extent will it (especially early on) be perceived as credible by market participants?[1] Although the statute provides for political independence of the ECB going formally beyond that of the Bundesbank, it will nevertheless be an institution that begins with no track record. And, as the current debate within ERM countries illustrates, outside pressure on the monetary authorities may remain considerable. Under these circumstances, the ECB is likely, at least initially, to lack some of the anti-inflation credibility of the established central banks— and especially of the Bundesbank.

---

[1] In many respects, the EMI can be expected to employ broadly similar monetary policy instruments as the Bundesbank, see EMI (1997). However, some important issues remain to be resolved, including whether the ECB will announce explicit operational targets for a monetary aggregate or inflation. These issues are also discussed in Moutot (1996).

Faced with potential market concerns about its anti-inflation resolve, the ECB may adopt policies to address this potential lack of credibility, and these policies themselves would affect economic conditions in countries inside and outside the EMU region. For example, the ECB could adopt a very tough policy line from the outset (that is, react strongly to excessive levels of inflation by tightening monetary policy). As emphasized in the literature on expectations formation and learning, good inflation outcomes would be a principal strategy for the central bank to establish its credibility,[2] which may entail short-run output costs until such credibility is established. Our paper attempts an analysis of the possible deflationary bias for the region.

Adopting initially a relatively tough policy stance to establish its anti-inflation credibility is but one of the possibilities for the new central bank. There are, however, several historical precedents for such a strategy. Examples include the early years of the Bundesbank itself, when it went well beyond what was required by the Bretton Woods system to establish its own anti-inflation reputation. Indeed, the relatively tight monetary stance (compared with partner countries) contributed to some of the imbalances that emerged under the Bretton Woods system and required, even before the system's demise, appreciations of the deutsche mark, including in 1961, 1969, and 1971 (Emminger, 1976). Another example of a relatively tight monetary policy stance in the wake of a monetary regime change is provided by the events following the decision of the U.S. Congress in 1875 to reintroduce (gold) convertibility. The Resumption Act of January 1875 stipulated the reintroduction of convertibility four years later, in January 1879, and, in the intervening years, the United States experienced considerable price deflation.[3] Against this historical background, it is of interest to investigate how the ECB, faced with initial concerns about its anti-inflation resolve, may act to overcome these market concerns.

We distinguish three groups of countries in our paper: those participating in EMU from the beginning (the ins); those not participating from the beginning, but joining an ERM-type exchange rate arrangement that ties their currencies to the euro (pre-ins); and those not joining EMU and pursuing an independent monetary policy (the outs). The latter group would include countries following their own inflation or monetary targeting, as undertaken currently, for example, in the United Kingdom or

---

[2]See, for example, Marcet and Sargent (1989). In the limit, an excessively "tough central banker" strategy would not be credible if it raised unemployment to a point that undermined all support for lowering inflation; see Isard and Laxton (1996).

[3]At the same time, real growth in these post-civil war years was also robust; see Friedman and Schwartz (1963).

Switzerland. We investigate the implications of different shocks and policy rules with the help of the IMF's multi-country macroeconomic model (MULTIMOD).[4] The macroeconomic analytical framework of MULTIMOD is based on a rational expectations extension of the classical Mundell-Fleming model.

Modeling EMU: Monetary Policy Regimes

Different monetary policy regimes can be expected to prevail depending on whether countries participate in EMU from the start, join an ERM-successor arrangement that ties their exchange rates to the euro, or stay out of both EMU as well as an ERM-successor arrangement. Following is a brief outline of the monetary policy regime envisaged for each of the three groups in the subsequent simulation exercises.

Monetary policy rule for the countries participating in EMU. We assume that the ECB will follow a monetary policy regime that would be broadly similar to that of the Bundesbank. Some of the details of implementing this framework, however, are likely to differ from the Bundesbank's implementation in the past, and these differences provide an interesting basis for the subsequent policy scenarios.

In a recent study, Clarida and Gertler (1996) show that the Bundesbank's policy may be captured reasonably well by a modified Taylor (1993) rule, where it sets short-term official interest rates based on a linear decision rule that weighs two components: deviations of expected inflation from the target rate, and deviations of output from "potential" (that is, a measure of the output gap). Their findings also suggest that the Bundesbank places an asymmetric weight on inflation depending on whether inflation is above or below the target, reacting more strongly in the case where inflation is expected to overshoot the target.

For the purpose of this study, we investigated how these features could be captured in a model such as MULTIMOD, which relies on annual data (as opposed to monthly data that formed the basis for most earlier studies). As it turns out, the Bundesbank's policy can be approximated by a rule where the central bank influences short-term interest rates by reacting to economic conditions in a manner that is similar to a modified Taylor rule à la Clarida and Gertler (1996). We assume the ECB follows a similar rule in influencing the short-term interest rate. Accordingly, like the Bundesbank, it would tend to respond more (or less) aggressively to deviations of inflation from target if inflation is ex-

---

[4]For a description of MULTIMOD's basic features—which include model-consistent expectations and separate blocks for each Group of Seven country and blocks for other industrial and developing countries—see Masson, Symansky, and Meredith (1990).

pected to be above (or below) the target rate. In terms of the monetary rule for the ECB, it takes into account the respective aggregate for all ins. Thus, for example, the output level and output gap will refer to the combined (weighted) values for all ins.

Monetary policy rule for countries participating in ERM–2 outside EMU. Some of the countries that will not participate in EMU are likely to join an ERM-successor arrangement ("ERM–2") that would explicitly relate their currencies to the euro. In the MULTIMOD simulations, we assume the main focal point for monetary policies in these countries would be an exchange rate policy rule similar to the one applied in the current version of MULTIMOD to non-German participants in the ERM (with the deutsche mark replaced by an EMU-wide currency aggregate, the euro, as the anchor currency). As a result, these countries will set their short-term interest rates according to a reaction function where short-term interest rates are adjusted to largely limit fluctuations of a country's exchange rate vis-à-vis the euro and its ERM–2 central parity rate.

Monetary policy rule for countries outside EMU and not participating in ERM–2. Countries that are neither participating in EMU nor in ERM–2 are assumed to follow an independent monetary policy. For simplicity, their monetary policy is modeled as following a money supply rule (see Masson, Symansky, and Meredith, 1990). An alternative would be an inflation target as the main guidepost for the monetary authorities; a future extension of our analysis would incorporate this possibility where appropriate, for example, in the case of the United Kingdom.

Anti-Inflation Credibility and a Tight Monetary Rule of the ECB: Simulation Results[5]

If the ECB encounters (or worries about) a possible lack of anti-inflation credibility, it may initially run a rather tight monetary policy to convince markets that it is serious about its inflation concern. As described earlier, there are several historical precedents for such a central bank strategy, and some of the possible implications are identified in the following simulation exercise[6]. In the simulations below, all shocks are unanticipated, and 1996 denotes the first year of each disturbance (that is, the initial period).

---

[5]Further details are provided in Krueger, Laxton, and Razin (1997), who also analyze possible additional implications of an initial lack of credibility for the ECB, including the effects of a portfolio preference shift away from the euro.

[6]Krueger, Laxton, and Razin (1997) also investigate other aspects of EMU, including the role of asymmtric shocks. Masson and Turtelboom (1997) also employ MULTIMOD, among others, to investigate the role of the euro as a reserve currency.

The IMF's standard version of MULTIMOD contains separate blocks for each of the Group of Seven countries, but all smaller industrial countries are lumped into one group. This set-up was preserved and the different grouping of countries undertaken is as follows: the ins are represented by France and Germany, which are modeled as following a common monetary policy rule as described earlier; the "pre-ins", that is, the countries whose monetary policy will be constrained by an ERM–2 exchange rate regime, will be exemplified by Italy; while the analysis of the outs, the independent monetary policy countries, will be approximated by the United Kingdom. Although these country-block representations present a considerable simplification, the analysis should still allow us to identify some basic qualitative features of EMU.

The set of simulations investigates the credibility issue raised earlier. To this end, two model set-ups are compared: a "high" credibility world, where the ECB follows the same policy rule as estimated for the Bundesbank (but focusing on euro-region-wide aggregates); and a "low" credibility world, where agents place a nonzero probability on a scenario in which the ECB would ease monetary conditions considerably and accommodate higher inflation.[7] However, to convince market participants that it is serious about its anti-inflation policy, the ECB would in this case react very strongly to any overrun in inflation relative to target. Specifically, we assume that the policy adjustment coefficient to anticipated inflation overruns is twice as large in this case as in the alternative scenario.[8] To examine the implications of the alternative model set-ups, we investigate in each case an expansionary government spending and investment shock in the EMU countries.[9] (See chart 1 for some of the results, depicting the difference between the two model set-ups.)

In the EMU countries, the positive demand shock raises output and inflation in the initial period. In the low credibility scenario, however, the monetary authority attempts to assert its anti-inflation determination and the ECB reacts strongly to the rise in inflation. As a result, nominal and

---

[7]Since the authorities are assumed to react strongly to dissuade these concerns (see below), it is assumed that the probability of the high inflation state reverts to zero after two periods (in the simulations, a .25 probability of a 10 percent inflation rate is assumed in the first two periods).

[8]The calibration of the respective reaction coefficient is similar to our estimates for a particular episode where the Federal Reserve undertook to re-establish its anti-inflation credentials. After a period of considerable acceleration in inflation, the Federal Reserve began to tighten monetary conditions sharply in the late 1970s and early 1980s, maintaining the tight stance until about the mid–1980s. Recursive estimates of a Taylor rule indicate roughly a doubling of the reaction coefficient for inflation above its target during this period.

[9]The investment shock is a temporary 10 percent increase in investment expenditure, lasting for two years, and a permanent 2 percent of GDP increase in government consumption expenditure in each EMU country.

Chart 1. Potential Effects of EMU: A Negative Demand Shock in France
(Difference between EMU and pre-EMU scenario; in percentage points)[1]

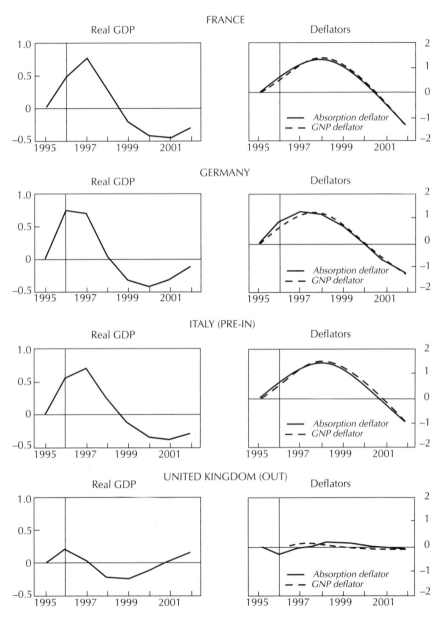

[1]See text for details.

real interest rates rise sharply, curtailing both investment and consumption demand. Compared with the high credibility scenario, short-term nominal interest rates rise by an additional 2 percentage points and real rates by even 3 percentage points, resulting in a relatively weaker level of activity. (See charts 1 and 2.) Moreover, the rise in interest rates leads to a nominal and real exchange rate appreciation in the low relative to the high credibility scenario, and a consequent weakening of the export performance. Only after the monetary authorities have re-established their credibility—assumed to take two years in these particular simulations—do the policy paths for these economies revert to the same equilibrium positions.

The differences between the low and high EMU credibility scenarios are broadly the same for the exchange-rate targeting pre-ins (Italy) as they are for the EMU participants. Accordingly, they follow the relative appreciation of the euro in the low credibility scenario and, combined with the increase in interest rates, this is accompanied by a temporary weakening in economic activity.

The effects on the outs (United Kingdom) are relatively small, with interest rates moving barely between the two scenarios. However, mirroring the exchange rate appreciation in other European countries, the exchange rate depreciates initially. But with the weakening in demand in continental Europe, this only cushions—it does not reverse—the negative effect on exports in the MULTIMOD simulations.

Conclusion

Our results illustrate that an initial lack of anti-inflation credibility for the ECB may introduce, in the short run, a deflationary bias for the EMU region. We show that when the ECB reacts in this environment to build its credibility, it will likely tighten monetary conditions severely if its policy target of price stability is in jeopardy. While highlighting the resulting deflationary bias, it is beyond this paper's scope to argue that this would be an inappropriate policy strategy for the ECB. Indeed, such strong actions in the short run may well be preferable, should the alternative result in persistent market doubts about the ECB's anti-inflation resolve; the latter result would likely entail high economic costs as illustrated by many historical episodes, including some during and after the periods of exchange market turbulence in the ERM system. But policy makers may have to preserve a fine balance, as "tough central banker" strategies that completely ignore the deflationary consequences of shocks and attempt to establish policy credibility too quickly may actually undermine the policy's success if the unemployment costs prove unacceptably high.

Chart 2. Lack of Full Credibility of the European Central Bank
(Difference between low- and high-credibility scenario; in percentage points.
Shocks: positive government spending and investment shock in EMU countries)[1]

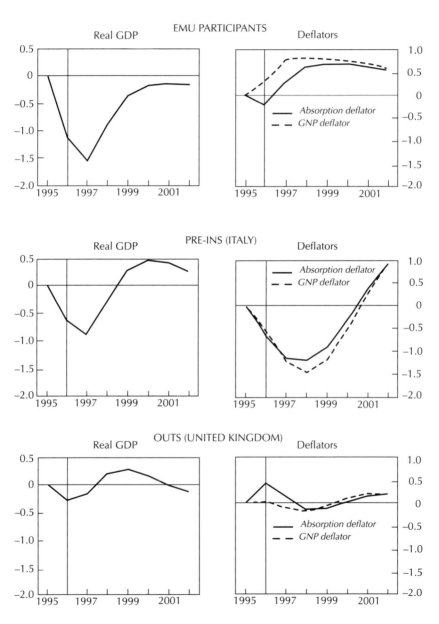

[1]See text for details.

References

Clarida, R. and M. Gertler, "How the Bundesbank Conducts Monetary Policy," NBER Working Paper, No. 5581 (May 1996), pp. 195–214.

Deutsche Bundesbank, *Monatsbericht,* Frankfurt, various issues.

Emminger, O., "Deutsche Geld- und Währungspolitik im Spannungsfeld zwischen innerem und äußerem Gleichgewicht (1948–1975)," in Deutsche Bundesbank, *Währung und Wirtschaft in Deutschland, 1876–1975,* Frankfurt (1976), pp. 485–554.

European Monetary Institute, *The Single Monetary Policy in Stage Three: Specification of the Operational Framework,* Frankfurt (1997).

Friedman, M. and A. J. Schwartz, *The Monetary History of the United States, 1867–1960,* Princeton University Press (1963).

Isard, P. and D. Laxton, "Strategic Choice in Phillips Curve Specification: What if Bob Gordon is Wrong?" paper presented at conference on European Unemployment: Macroeconomic Aspects, in Florence (November 29–30, 1996).

Krueger, T., D. Laxton and A. Razin, "European Union and the Macroeconomic Effects of Alternative Monetary Policy Rules: A Deflationary Bias?" mimeo, Washington (1997).

Marcet, A. and T. J. Sargent, "Convergence of Least-Squares Learning in Environments with Hidden State Variables and Private Information," *Journal of Political Economy,* 97 (December 1989), pp. 1306–22.

Masson, P. R., S. Symansky, and G. Meredith, *MULTIMOD Mark II: A Revised and Extended Model,* Occasional Paper No. 71, International Monetary Fund (1990).

Masson, P. R. and B. Turtelboom, "Characteristics of the Euro, the Demand for Reserves, and Policy Coordination under EMU," paper presented at Conference on EMU and the International Monetary System, Washington (March 17–18, 1997).

Moutot, P., "Monetary Policy in a European Union: Instruments, Strategy and Transmission Mechanism," paper presented at Conference on Monetary Policy in Transition, Vienna (November 17–19, 1996).

Taylor, J., "Discretion versus Policy Rules in Practice," Carnegie Rochester Conference on Public Policy (December 1993), pp. 195–214.

The Credibility Problem, EMU and Swedish Monetary Policy*

Alex Cukierman

L IMITED CREDIBILITY INCREASES the likelihood of financial crises, raises the employment costs of stabilization policy and the cost of capital to government, and generally reduces the allocative efficiency of the capital market. My paper surveys current conventional wisdom concerning the institutions conducive to maintaining a stable internal and external value of the currency and applies its lessons to the current Swedish situation. The paper's basic premise is that Swedish monetary policy should be directed mostly to the twin objectives of achieving and maintaining price stability and a high level of credibility. The paper poses the question of whether Sweden should join a European monetary union, if such a union is created, or whether it should try to maintain price stability and credibility by other means.

Limited credibility means that unions, investors in the capital market, and the general public are relatively skeptical about the commitment of policy makers to price stability. As a consequence, when—despite those suspicions—monetary policy is geared mainly to achieving price stability, realized inflation is lower than expected inflation. As a result, ex post real interest rates are higher than ex ante rates, which increases the likelihood of financial crises. In addition, given nominal wage contracts, ex post real wages are higher than expected, which reduces employment, economic activity, and the country's external competitiveness.

My paper discusses the costs of limited credibility and the relative merits of alternative credibility-building institutions, the reasons for Sweden's past poor credibility record, and prospects for the formation of

*The full paper appears in the Spring 1997 issue of *Swedish Economic Policy Review* (English).

a monetary union. I also evaluate alternative possible reforms of monetary institutions. My recommendation is for Swedish policy makers to reform domestic monetary and fiscal institutions in ways that would enhance Sweden's commitment to price stability and try to abide by the Maastricht criteria in order to leave open the option of joining a monetary union. In particular, I emphasize that the legal independence of the Swedish Riksbank should be upgraded. Such a course of action is advisable independently of whether Sweden ultimately decides to join or not.

The decision on whether or not to join a monetary union can be viewed as an attempt to pick the point most suitable for Sweden along a credibility—flexibility trade-off. Because of current uncertainties regarding the composition of the union—its basic rules and the time of its formation—the decision to join corresponds to a relatively wide range of points along this trade-off. One advantage of building credibility at home by reforming monetary and fiscal institutions is that it makes it possible to choose the point along the credibility-flexibility trade-off with higher accuracy. Whether joining the union will enhance Swedish credibility more or less than if credibility were produced at home obviously depends on the type of domestic reforms and on the future form of the union. One advantage of joining is that it automatically maintains Sweden's relative credibility level. A low level of relative credibility was largely responsible for Sweden's 1992 foreign exchange crisis.

The paper's recommendation takes into consideration not only the need to boost credibility, but also the uncertainty surrounding the formation of a monetary union and its precise structure, as well as prospects for some resolution of this uncertainty in the foreseeable future. The paper also contains a general discussion of the effects of non-transparent, or opaque, policy procedures on the evolution of credibility when monetary policy is also used for anticyclical purposes. Opaque policy procedures increase the public's uncertainty about the determination of policy makers to achieve price stability. In most countries, monetary policy is not fully committed to price stability, nor is it totally discretionary. But in many countries, the degree of commitment fluctuates over time and is therefore not known with certainty by unions, financial market participants, and the general public.

As a consequence, when policy makers in such countries pursue stabilization policy, the public rationally attributes part of the associated fluctuations in inflation and money growth to changes in the commitment of policy to price stability, as well as to stabilization attempts.

The larger the public's uncertainty about the degree of commitment to price stability, the larger the effect of changes in the rate of inflation on the credibility of this commitment. The reason is that (given the variance of the real shocks to be stabilized) the larger the uncertainty about the strength of the commitment, the more likely that a given change in the inflation rate is due to a change in the degree of commitment, rather than to an attempt to stabilize the economy. The level of uncertainty about the commitment to price stability is determined by the structure of institutions in charge of monetary policy. I refer to institutions that clearly reveal the degree of commitment to the public as "transparent" and to those that do not as "opaque." An appendix to the paper demonstates that, with transparent monetary institutions, countercyclical monetary policy has a smaller impact on credibility than under more opaque institutions.

To llustrate this general principle, suppose some real shocks temporarily reduce the natural level of employment below its mean value and that—since monetary policy is countercyclical—this induces an increase in the rate of inflation. Consider now two countries with the *same* shocks and with *identical* policy responses but with different transparencies of monetary institutions. Inflation expectations in both countries will rise and both will suffer some credibility loss. But this loss will be smaller in the country with more transparent monetary institutions. The other side of the coin is that when natural employment is above trend, and money growth therefore below trend, the country with more opaque policy procedures will gain more credibility. But if cyclical fluctuations are symmetric ex ante, it appears preferable to divorce stabilization policy from fluctuations in the credibility of monetary policy.

The Two Concepts of Money, and the Future of Europe

C.A.E. Goodhart

I. On the Nature and Origins of Money

THERE HAS BEEN A CONTINUING DEBATE between those who argue that a currency's value is based essentially on the power of the issuing authority ("Cartalists") and those who argue that the value depends primarily, or solely, on the intrinsic value of the backing of that currency ("Metallists"). An associated debate exists between those who have argued that money evolved as a private-sector, market-oriented response to overcoming the transactions costs inherent in barter—call them "Mengerians," after Karl Menger (1892), who anticipated most of the more formal subsequent models by such economists as Brunner (1971), Alchian (1977) and, more recently, Kiyotaki and Wright (1989)—and those who argue that the state has played a central role in the evolution and establishment of money.

The "M" team has assembled the more illustrious collection of economists—not to mention the endorsement of Aristotle. The "C" team, in contrast, has arrayed a more motley and fringe group of economists, including Mireaux in France (1930), and (most) U.S. and U.K. post-Keynesians. Nevertheless, the C-team approach has also won the support of a sizable majority of those in other disciplines—including anthropologists, numismatists, and historians concerned with the origin of money. Whereas the M group has been strong on formal theory, it has been constitutionally weak on historical empiricism, with such few exceptions as Melitz (1974).

Thus, in view of the severe transactions costs of barter, many economists have constructed models showing how the private sector could evolve toward a monetary economy as a function of a search for cost minimization procedures within a private-sector system, in which government does not necessarily enter at all.

Precious metals, with their advantages—such as durability, divisability, and portability—first became generally used as a means of payment and medium of exchange. Yet in their raw state, it is difficult to identify and confirm their fineness and quality. The thrust of Alchian's paper (1977), however, is that money arises as a result of the existence of a good with low identification costs. But the costs of identifying the quality of either unworked or fabricated precious metals for the ordinary person is probably considerably higher, for example, than the cost of identifying the value of items in everyday use—such as salt, corn, nails, or even perhaps cattle (most people in a rural agricultural community would, however, be able to assess the value of a cow)—and again greater than the value of an item acceptable by being needed for certain intra-societal functions (for example, religious or wergeld).

This may appear to be a straw man. Few people have argued that precious metals would be used as a medium-of-exchange currency, until the identification problem was largely resolved by the technical innovation of a mint process whereby the identification costs could be drastically reduced by stamping a quality guarantee upon a coin. Thus, the argument is that a combination of the innate characteristics of precious metals, plus the identification cost reduction permitted by minting, enabled the private sector to evolve toward a monetary system.

But to suggest that this all occurred purely within the private sector is historically flawed. Although, once the idea and technical process is discovered, minting would seem to be as capable of being accomplished by the private sector as any other metalworking process, in practice minting has, in the vast majority of cases, been a public-sector operation. In those cases where the mint has been privately run, the government has in most cases set both the standards of fineness and a rent, or seigniorage tax, that extracted most of the available profits.

Minting came under the government's aegis for two associated reasons. First, a mint requires an inventory of precious metals, which attracts opportunistic theft and violence. Minting requires protection, and the protector (wielding the force necessary to maintain law and order in the economic system) will be able to extract most of the rent from the system. Second, the costs of identifying the true value (quality) of the metal included in the minted coin leads to time inconsistency. The mint operator is bound to claim that that quality will be maintained; in practice, the operator will be tempted to debase the currency in pursuit of a quick and immediately larger return. Olson (1997) describes how the development of a secure, dynastic regime reduces time inconsistency in the ruler.

Under the M-form theory, the collapse of stable government would have no relevance, or impact, on the quality of the currency (money) used. Under the C-form theory, the quality of money and the stability of the government are closely interlinked. History supports the C-form theory. The M-form theory has difficulty in accounting for the jump from a metallic-based currency to a fiat, paper-based currency. The C-form theory has no such difficulty.

I conclude that the inter-relationship between the governance structure of the economy, the form and usage of money (and also taxes in a three-way interactive relationship), is essential. The attempt to model the evolution of money in a model without government (or taxation) may be intellectually rewarding but is historically and practically invalid.

II. The M-Form Spatial Theory, or Optimum Currency Areas

If the use of money can evolve through a search process of cost minimization, without any necessary intervention by a government, by analogous reasoning, the spatial domain for any one money can also evolve from such a similar cost-minimization search process. The optimum currency area analysis has, indeed, followed this approach; it has broadly compared the benefit, in terms of transaction cost minimization, of having a single currency over a wider area with the cost in terms of adjustment difficulty.

Under optimum currency area (OCA) theory, currency domains do not need to be coincident and coterminous with sovereign states. There is no reason why such a state should not have any number of currencies from zero to n, and an optimal currency area, in turn, should be able, in theory, to incorporate (parts of) any number of separate countries from one to n. Under the M-form OCA theory, currency areas and the boundaries of sovereign states should be divorced.

The reverse is, of course, true for the C-form theory. Since under this theory money is so intimately bound up with the stable existence and fiscal functions of government in any area, the sovereign government of that area should maintain its single currency within that area's boundaries.

Which theory has the better predictive and explanatory power? Eichengreen (1996) writes,

"Michael Mussa is fond of describing how, each time he walks to the IMF cafeteria, down the corridor where the currency notes of the member states are arrayed, he rediscovers one of the most robust regularities of monetary economics: the one-to-one correspondence between countries and currencies. If monetary unification precedes political unification in Europe, it will be an unprecedented event."

In practice, of course, virtually all empirical work on OCA, in contrast with the original theory (for example, of Mundell), has taken the coincidence of the nation state and its separate currency as the initial starting point, usually without noticing that this coincidence is explicable only under C-form theory. Such work goes on to discuss currency unification across several nation states—for example, in the European Union—or separation—for example, Quebec—without full appreciation, in most cases, that under C-form theory, the key factors must be the future political relationships between various levels of government and the monetary authority.

Perhaps the clearest indication of the comparative predictive and explanatory power of the C-form theory comes on the occasion of the break-up of existing federations into separate states, as in the recent case of the U.S.S.R., Czechoslovakia, Yugoslavia or Austro-Hungary after World War I, or, on the other hand, of the unification of smaller states into a larger federal state—as in the founding ofthe United States, Germany, or Australia. The C-form theory predicts that the fragmentation of sovereignty will lead to a fragmentation into separate currencies, while unification into an effective federal state will lead to unification of previously separate currencies. The M-form theory has nothing useful to offer on this. If the U.S.S.R. was an optimum currency area before its break-up, it should have been one afterward. Similarly, if Prussia and Bavaria had been OCAs before the unification of Germany, they should presumably have remained so afterward.

Two qualifications apply to the above argument. First, a sovereign government imposes laws and encourages behavior (for example, use of a single dominant language) that usually help make labor markets far more flexible within, than between, such countries. Second, the role of the unified federal fiscal system helps mitigate idiosyncratic shocks in the constituent member states. Note that neither qualification will apply under European economic and monetary union! What is remarkable, and virtually unique, about the proposed move to EMU and the euro is that it will be done without an accompanying federalization of governmental and fiscal functions.

III. Fiscal Limits Within EMU

Within nation states the domestic debt of the sovereign debtor—that is, central government bonds—always has the highest possible credit rating (AAA) because it has no credit risk, apart from political collapse. This is because the government has had the power to use its authority, through its central bank, in a pinch if necessary, to create money to pay off such nominal liabilities. This, of course, has the downside that the government may be tempted into imprudent fiscal and monetary policies that can, and do, create inflation and exchange rate risks. It is partly to reduce these latter risks that the single currency and the obligation of an independent European central bank to give priority to price stability have been promulgated.

All this is fair enough, but it leaves unanswered the question of how the national fiscal authorities will be affected once they lose the crutch of national money-creating powers. I contend that this divorce will significantly weaken their position. If so, the fiscal criteria of Maastricht and the Waigel pact obtain stronger backing, and might even need further tightening.

Apart from the participating nation states' inability with EMU to vary (control is too strong a word) their revenue from seigniorage and their taxes on their banking systems, they will lose their former ability to use their money-creating powers to pay off their domestic currency debts, interest, and principal in legal tender, whatever the market conditions.

All this must change with the move to a single currency under EMU. The authorities lose their ability to inflate away the real value of their national debt; indeed, this is partly the purpose of the exercise. But what if there is a drop in demand in the bond market for national debt? Governments could previously have halted declining bond prices and rising interest rates by monetizing the debt. After EMU, they will no longer be able to do so. Moreover, a run on the bond market in such conditions becomes rapidly self-reinforcing, a vicious spiral. The higher interest rates worsen the fiscal outlook (unambiguously in the absence of seigniorage), which reduces bond demand. This, in turn, raises interest rates, which worsens the fiscal outlook. The possibility for a self-sustaining run in bond markets would seem even more serious than in the case of foreign exchange markets. EMU will abolish exchange rate disturbances and inflation differentials between members, and should thereby eliminate associated interest rate differentials. But will this be at the expense of greater bond market disturbances and interest rate differentials based on relative credit risk? How serious might these latter be?

Without associated central banks, national debt markets will assume the characteristics of those markets for public-sector debt wherein the borrower cannot itself directly create money. Two main categories of borrowers of this kind already exist, in the guise of the foreign currency debt of sovereign states and the debt market for subsidiary states, for example, the individual U.S. states. Liquidity risks in such cases tend to place more severe restrictions on the capacity of borrowers to raise debt, even more severely than solvency considerations. For example, sovereign states normally maintain much lower ratios of foreign currency to national currency debt.

At a recent discussion in which I participated, executives from a rating agency intimated that they expected the best guide to the credit rating of the national bonds of the participating countries would be the existing ratings of their current foreign currency debt. When I pointed out that the relevant ratios, of debt and debt-service-to-GDP, would, after EMU, become instantaneously far worse (than the current foreign currency debt ratios), there was no clear response. One suggestion was that, if not the European central bank, other countries might come to the aid of a member state facing adverse debt market conditions, perhaps to prevent exactly the same kind of contagion that eventually overwhelmed the exchange rate mechanism of the European Monetary System.

The main protection against liquidity crises is either to reassure the lender by collateralizing the debt, or to limit debt and debt service to a level that can easily be paid off by a feasible and relatively quick adjustment in cash flows. Despite some suggestions that sovereign foreign currency debt of states failing to meet interest payment commitments could be met by seizing and selling public-sector assets either within, or without, the physical boundaries of those states, this route does not appear promising. So, the main protection against liquidity crises must presumably be met by restricting debt and debt service to levels payable by a plausible and reasonably rapid change in cash flows, if pressed.

Eichengreen and von Hagen (1995) are absolutely correct in principle when they comment that the debt position of U.S. states and local governments needs to be much more constrained than that of member states participating in EMU. This is because the former have much less ability to improve their cash flow, at times of crisis, by raising taxes or reducing spending. This argument is correct, but Eichengreen and von Hagen go on to claim that,

> "In Europe, the EU has only limited taxation and expenditure authority. The vast majority of taxation remains under the control of member states. This is certain to remain so for the foreseeable future. All this suggests that the rationale for the Excessive Deficits Procedure is weak."

This does not follow, however, because what matters is the ratio between debt service requirements and the borrower's ability to adjust its cash flow. Certainly the latter is lower in U.S. states, but so also is the former. The data on the debt service, outstanding debt, and operating primary surplus/deficit of U.S. states are vastly stronger than that for EU countries. The U.S. state with the lowest credit rating in 1994 (Louisiana, Baa1) had a debt per capita of $895, debt service as a percent of revenues of 11½ percent, and an operating surplus of $311 per capita. By comparison, the figures for Germany and Italy were debt per capita of $9,026 and $21,020, respectively; debt service of 17.8 percent and 50.0 percent; and a deficit of $413 and $1,543! If Louisiana debt is rated only Baa1, what should be the proper rating for member EU states?

Thus, the effective removal of central banks from participating member states within EMU may expose them to serious fragility and credit risk in their bond markets. Although this view has been adopted by a few C-form commentators, M-form theorists have not treated it seriously, nor, it would appear, has the market. Data from the swaps market, for example, suggest that the credit risk on Belgian government debt is being priced at 8–10 basis points (despite a debt service ratio of more than 45 percent of GDP!). Moreover, the main current feature in European debt markets is a convergence play, whereby bond yields are revised downward toward German bund yield levels dependent on their probability of entry in 1999. If my arguments are correct, the convergence play has been massively overdone, if not altogether wrong-headed.

The same argument suggests that a default (on its interest payments) of a member state within EMU is a real possibility, assuming the no-bail-out clause sticks. The main danger to the country involved, and to the EU, would then be a subsequent financial contagious collapse of some sizable part of the financial (banking) sector. Sensible, realistic capital asset ratios need to be imposed on bank holdings of participating member state bonds from January 1, 1999. But beyond this, the default of any participating member state would have an immediate and severe effect on the debt markets of several other member states, if these are feared to be in any similar position (similar to the "tequila effect").

This represents a rationale for adopting, and adhering strictly to, the Waigel pact. The implications for demand management and unemployment within EMU in the next few years, therefore, look highly deflationary. This is partly a consequence of divorcing the fiscal and monetary authorities from each other's embrace.

References

Alchian, A, "Why Money?" *Journal of Money, Credit and Banking,* 9 (1), Part 2 (February 1977), pp. 133–40.
Brunner, K., "The Uses of Money: Money in the Theory of an Exchange Economy," *American Economc Review,* 61 (5), (December 1971).
Eichengreen, B., "A More Perfect Union? The Logic of Economic Integration," Essays in International Finance, No. 198 (June 1996).
Eichengreen, B. and J. von Hagen, "Fiscal Policy and Monetary Union: Federalism, Fiscal Restrictions and the No-Bail-Out Rule," CEPR Discussion Paper Series, No. 1247 (September 1995).

Kyotaki, N. and R. Wright, "On Money as a Medium of Exchange," *Journal of Political Economy,* 97 (4) (August 1989), pp. 927–54.
Menger, K., "On the Origin of Money," *Economic Journal* (1892).
Melitz, J., *Primitive and Modern Money: An Interdisciplinary Approach* (Reading, Mass: Addison-Wesley Publishing, 1974).
Mireaux, E., *Les Miracles du Credit,* Editions des Portigues (Paris, 1930).
Olson, M., *Capitalism, Socialism and Dictatorship,* preliminary transcript (Maryland University, 1997).

Debt-Creating Versus Nondebt-Creating Fiscal Stabilization Policies: Ricardian Equivalence, Fiscal Stabilization, and EMU

Tamim Bayoumi and Paul R. Masson

PLANS TO CREATE A SINGLE EUROPEAN CURRENCY have generated work in many areas of economics, as researchers try to assess both the implications and advisability of this undertaking. One of these has been the operation of fiscal stabilizers. Without the monetary flexibility provided by separate currencies, labor mobility, wage flexibility, and fiscal stabilizers all represent potentially important ways of reducing the impact of idiosyncratic cyclical disturbances across regions of the projected currency union. The function of fiscal stabilization policies in monetary unions has already generated an extensive academic literature, going back to the original paper on optimum currency areas by Robert Mundell. In the European context, it has also been the subject of an official report in the late 1970s. More recently, the European Community Commission has published a collection of papers devoted to the fiscal requirements for the successful operation of European economic and monetary union (EMU).

The recent debate in Europe on the role of fiscal stabilizers after EMU has not, however, focused on the appropriate size of fiscal stabilizers, important though it may be. Rather, the central issue has been the level of government that should be used to operate them. Within existing national currency unions, most fiscal stabilization is carried out at the national (federal) level, rather than at lower levels of government. Empirical estimates of the size of federal fiscal stabilizers within the United States and other countries generally find them to be significant—with fiscal flows offsetting as much as 20–30 percent of the initial reduction in income. As far as EMU is concerned, the logical counterpart to this behavior within countries would be to give a significant role in fiscal stabilization to a central authority of the union. This is not, however, the approach that the European Union (EU) countries intend to adopt, with several of them resisting any moves toward federalism. Rather, fiscal stabilization within the new currency union will be carried out primarily at the level of the nation state.

The question arises whether the level of government at which fiscal stabilization occurs has any effect on its net impact. We argue there are good reasons for believing there is such a difference. When local governments provide fiscal stabilization within their own region there is a direct impact on the level of local government debt. To the extent that citizens take account of the future tax liabilities implicit in this increase in debt in their current saving decisions, they will partially offset the fiscal boost provided by the government. If a federal government provides stabilization across a number of regions all experiencing different disturbances, however, the impact on federal debt will tend to cancel out; there will be no expectation of future tax liabilities, and, hence, less of a private sector offset to fiscal stabilization.

The issue is best seen in the context of the Ricardian equivalence proposition. In the extreme case of complete Ricardian equivalence, local governments are unable to provide fiscal stabilization within their locality, as their actions will be offset by the private sector due to expectations of higher future taxes. To the extent that deficits across differing regions cancel out, however, federal governments *can* provide fiscal stabilization across regions (although not for the economy as a whole) as fiscal insurance is being provided across regions rather than across time. The same logic can be used to argue that federal stabilizers will be more effective than local ones, even in worlds in which Ricardian effects are only partial, unless the shocks they respond to are perfectly correlated and the regional cycles perfectly synchronized, which is unlikely. Again, the impact of a local deficit on future taxes is smaller, and hence so is the Ricardian offset. As the members of EMU lose the ability to use their exchange rate to combat intra-regional disturbances, the size of fiscal multipliers clearly becomes more important.

The implication of the analysis for EMU is that stabilization by national governments is likely to produce less bang for the same buck than an equivalent EU-wide policy. While the sign of the effect is unambiguous, however, its potential size is unclear. Existing estimates of the size of the Ricardian offset to fiscal policy, and, hence, the potential increase in the stabilization bang from a federal policy, vary widely. We look at this issue directly using data on fiscal policy across differing levels of government for the Canadian provinces. We contrast the impact of changes in federal fiscal deficits on private consumption with that of changes in fiscal deficits by lower levels of government. Our results indicate that idiosyncratic shocks are cushioned more effectively by federal fiscal policy that is nondebt-creating, that is, that involves a degree of redistribution across provinces.

Our empirical results thus confirm that the anticipated larger impact on consumption of fiscal deficits that do not create debt compared with deficits that do appears to hold empirically. In all cases, the two coefficients are significantly different from each other. Most estimates imply that debt-creating deficits are somewhat less than half as effective as nondebt-creating ones. Although we (barely) reject Ricardian equivalence for the debt-creating policies, our much stronger result is that stabilization policy within a federal system that involves some degree of redistribution is far more effective in cushioning shocks to consumption.

Policy Implications

We interpret this evidence as providing a further argument for Europe to consider expanding fiscal policy at the union level, rather than relying on national fiscal policies to offset idiosyncratic shocks. As pointed out by others, effective fiscal stabilization is all the more important in EMU, given the loss of the exchange rate instrument for that purpose— especially since other shock absorbers, such as labor mobility, are unlikely to be available. One also needs to acknowledge, however, important design problems in implementing fiscal stabilization at the EU level that would not involve important persistent transfers of revenue from some countries to others, as well as more general issues of sovereignty. Moreover, since in practice taxes are not lump sum, the distorting effects of higher tax rates also need to be taken into account.

Monetary Union Without Fiscal Coordination May Discipline Policy Makers

Roel M. W. J. Beetsma and A. Lans Bovenberg

RECENT DEVELOPMENTS IN THE STATES of the former Soviet Union and, in particular, plans for European monetary unification have attracted renewed interest in the study of common currency areas. Such areas are often characterized by a large number of decentralized fiscal authorities, which fail to take into account potential externalities on other fiscal authorities in the same area. Other examples of common currency areas with many decentralized fiscal authorities are such federal countries as Brazil, Argentina, and the former Yugoslavia.

Some recent work suggests that a monetary union with decentralized fiscal decision making produces an inflationary bias and excessive public spending (Aizenman, 1992). This lack of monetary and fiscal discipline in a monetary union would provide a case for fiscal coordination (see, for example, Krichel, Levine, and Pearlman, 1994). Moreover, several researchers find that the attractiveness of entering a monetary union or admitting a new participant decreases with the number of participants (see, for example, Alesina and Grilli, 1993).

We argue that monetary unification without coordination among decentralized fiscal authorities may actually reduce the inflation bias and the bias toward public spending. These reductions are larger, the larger the number of union participants. Admitting new participants may therefore raise welfare throughout the union.

We set up a simple model of a monetary union with a common central bank (CCB) and decentralized fiscal authorities. In concluding nominal wage contracts, the private sector acts as a Stackelberg leader against the policy authorities. In setting tax rates, the fiscal authorities are in turn a leader vis-à-vis the CCB, which is unable to commit to announcements of low future inflation. The CCB is independent in the sense that it does not take into account the budget constraints of the individual governments when setting the inflation rate. Such a CCB could correspond to the European central bank (ECB), which would be explicitly forbidden to receive instructions from governments or to finance government deficits. After the CCB sets the inflation rate, public spending is set to balance the government budget. This description of fiscal-monetary interaction seems realistic because tax rates cannot be adjusted as quickly as monetary policy, so that a particular choice of tax rates provides the government with a first-mover advantage.

Social welfare losses depend on deviations of inflation, output, and public spending from their target levels. If policy makers share the objectives of society but lack commitment, insular policy making (that is policy making at the national level outside a monetary union) produces undisciplined policies. In particular, inflation, public spending, and taxes are all excessive from a social perspective. Intuitively, discretionary policy uses unanticipated inflation, which is self-defeating in equilibrium, as an indirect instrument to alleviate tax distortions. By raising the tax rate, the fiscal authorities force the CCB into raising the inflation rate to protect employment. The resulting higher tax and seigniorage revenues imply a bias toward excessive spending.

In fact, this spending bias arises from two possible sources of conflict between the fiscal and monetary authorities. One source is the failure of the CCB to internalize the government budget constraint; the other is a conflict between the monetary and fiscal authorities about the inflation objectives. Monetary unification, or increasing a union of a given size, alleviates the resulting lack of discipline. This is because a large union containing many noncooperating fiscal players strengthens the strategic position of the CCB, which favors lower inflation because it does not internalize the beneficial impact of unanticipated inflation in relaxing government budget constraints. The spending bias vanishes completely if the number of countries rises to infinity, or if the CCB is made ultraconservative (the relative weight it attaches to low and stable inflation goes to infinity). In that case, each government realizes that its individual influence on the CCB's policies is negligible, so that the incentive to raise taxes to affect the CCB's inflation policy vanishes completely.

With benevolent policy makers (that is, policy makers who share society's preferences) and not-too-large base money holdings, an increase in the size of the union raises welfare in two ways: It reduces the spending bias, which improves the tax-spending mix, and it reduces inflation. This enhances welfare in modern economies in which small holdings of base money limit the adverse implications of lower inflation for seigniorage revenues. If policy makers are not benevolent, the welfare effects depend on whether inflation is initially too high or too low. The former case prevails if the CCB is not too conservative. The increased size of the union pushes inflation down in the direction of its social optimum, thereby enhancing welfare.

Failure to commit to a pre-announced monetary policy generally implies a suboptimal equilibrium. The recent literature has identified several institutional solutions to the problems associated with discretionary monetary policymaking. Rogoff (1985) suggests the appointment of a central banker who puts a larger relative weight on low and stable inflation than the representative agent does. The optimal degree of central bank "conservatism" eliminates part of the inflation bias, at the cost, however, of a suboptimal response to supply-side shocks. Hence, there is a trade-off between credibility and flexibility. Walsh (1995) shows that this trade-off is unnecessary if the central banker is given a contract that imposes the appropriate punishment for too-high inflation. Such a contract eliminates the inflation bias completely without sacrificing efficient stabilization. The problem with the contracting approach is that such contracts are hardly ever observed in practice. A more common approach is to impose an inflation target on the central bank, as in, for example, the United Kingdom, Canada, and New Zealand. Svensson (1995) shows that the optimal inflation target yields the same optimal equilibrium as the optimal contract.

We investigate these suggestions for dealing with the absence of commitment in our model. In contrast to the above-mentioned papers, we exclude shocks. In the context of their models, the trade-off between credibility and flexibility would then vanish and each of the three arrangements discussed above would yield the same equilibrium in which the inflation bias is completely eliminated. Of course, our model differs from previous models because we assign an explicit role for fiscal policy. In particular, inflation is a source of seigniorage revenues, and a way to reduce the real value of outstanding debt. Therefore, despite the absence of shocks, the three institutional arrangements are no longer equivalent. In particular, while the targeting and contracting approaches are still equivalent, appointing a conservative central banker leads to different results.

If both monetary and fiscal objectives can be adjusted, the second best can be reached by making the CCB sufficiently conservative (Rogoff, 1985) and the fiscal authorities even more conservative (that is, more inflation averse) than the CCB. However, the CCB should not be made ultraconservative (that is, given a mandate exclusively for price stability) if money holdings are positive, because it is optimal to have some inflation to raise seigniorage revenues. The fiscal authorities should be made even more conservative than the CCB because, in contrast to the CCB, they do internalize the benefits of inflation in terms of seigniorage revenues and lower debt service costs. They should therefore be provided with a stronger disincentive to push for higher inflation. If the union's size goes to infinity, the second best is reached only by making the CCB ultraconservative.

Because the fiscal authorities are subject to daily political pressure, it seems more realistic to assume that their objectives cannot be adjusted. In the special case where the fiscal authorities do not care about inflation at all, the CCB should be made even more conservative to offset the inflationary pressure exerted by such fiscal authorities. Where fiscal authorities are benevolent, we have to resort to numerical simulations. An increase in union size, while optimally adjusting the CCB, is welfare-enhancing. In fact, the problem of not being able to adjust fiscal objectives is smaller in a larger union, because the benefits—as perceived by an individual fiscal authority—of exerting pressure on the CCB are smaller.

Because the outcomes for any given linear contract can be replicated by the appropriate inflation target, we discuss only the case of inflation targets. A lower inflation target boosts public spending. This is because it reduces the inflation rate preferred by the CCB relative to the rate preferred by the fiscal authorities. Therefore the fiscal authorities raise taxes, as higher taxes induce the CCB to raise inflation to protect employment. The large tax and seigniorage revenues boost public spending. The second best can be reached again, however, provided both monetary and fiscal objectives are adjusted appropriately.

If it is not possible to adjust fiscal preferences, imposing a lower target creates a trade-off between lower inflation and a larger spending bias. The effect of a target on spending vanishes only if the fiscal authorities do not care about inflation at all. The inflation target should then be set lower than if fiscal preferences cannot be adjusted. Intuitively, given that the fiscal authorities do not care about inflation, they will exert pressure on the CCB to produce more inflation. A lower inflation target is needed to provide the CCB with a stronger incentive to keep inflation low. If real money holdings are zero, the target is set consistent with the socially optimal inflation rate of zero. Yet because the tax-spending mix is still suboptimal, the second best is not achieved. An increase in the union size mitigates the spending bias and enhances welfare.

As mentioned above, if fiscal objectives can also be adjusted, both the optimal target and an optimally designed, conservative central bank will yield the second best. If fiscal objectives cannot be adjusted, the two arrangements yield different outcomes. With zero money holdings, making the central bank ultraconservative is preferred to the optimal inflation target. While the former solution achieves the second best, the latter still implies a suboptimal tax spending mix and, thus, a suboptimal equilibrium. The reason is that the response of the inflation rate to a marginal increase in taxes is unaffected, even with an optimal inflation target. Governments will still have the incentive to set taxes too high to force the CCB to produce more inflation.

For the more general case of positive money holdings, we resort to numerical results. Assuming that fiscal authorities are benevolent, the optimally designed, conservative CCB is generally associated with lower welfare losses than the optimal inflation target. The differences in welfare losses are relatively large for small unions, but become very small for larger unions.

With fiscal policy coordination, each fiscal player internalizes the effects of its actions on the other fiscal players. The benefits of raising taxes for the purpose of higher inflation are correspondingly higher. Fiscal coordination thus strengthens the strategic position of the fiscal authorities against the CCB and leads to the same outcomes as national policy making outside a monetary union. Hence, fiscal coordination eliminates the disciplining and potentially welfare-enhancing effects of monetary unification. This provides an argument for applying the subsidiarity principle to fiscal policy making within a monetary union.

References

Aizenman, J., "Competitive Externalities and the Optimal Seigniorage," *Journal of Money, Credit, and Banking*, 24, pp. 61–71 (1992).

———, "Soft Budget Constraints, Taxes, and the Incentive to Cooperate," *International Economic Review*, 34, pp. 819–32 (1992).

Alesina, A. and V. U. Grilli, "On the Feasibility of a One or Multi-Speed European Monetary Union," NBER Working Paper No. 4350 (1993).

Krichel, T., Levine, P., and J. Pearlman, "Fiscal and Monetary Policy in a Monetary Union: Credible Inflation Targets or Monetised Debt?" mimeo, University of Surrey (1994).

Rogoff, K., "The Optimal Degree of Commitment to an Intermediate Monetary Target," *Quarterly Journal of Economics*, 99, 1169–89 (1985).

Svensson, L.E.O., "Optimal Inflation Targets, 'Conservative' Central Banks, and Linear Inflation Contracts," CEPR Discussion Paper, No. 1249 (1995).

Walsh, C., "Optimal Contracts for Independent Central Bankers," *American Economic Review*, Vol. 85, No. 1, pp.150–67 (1995).

International Risk Sharing and European
Monetary Unification

Bent E. Sørensen and Oved Yosha

ECHANISMS FOR ACHIEVING INCOME insurance and consumption smoothing are essential for the stability of a monetary union. Without such mechanisms, countries in recession will have an incentive to leave the economic union. Central fiscal institutions can provide cross-country income insurance via a tax-transfer system and by allocating grants to the governments of specific countries. Market institutions can also provide risk sharing. The members of a union can share risk via cross-ownership of productive assets, facilitated by a developed capital market; they may smooth their consumption by adjusting their asset portfolio in response to shocks, for example, through lending and borrowing on international credit markets. In previous work, jointly with P.F. Asdrubali, we found that in the United States—a successful monetary union—62 percent of shocks to the per capita gross product of individual states are smoothed on average through transactions on markets, 13 percent are smoothed by the federal tax-transfer and grant system, and 25 percent are not smoothed. Therefore, although perfect insurance is not achieved, there is considerable risk sharing among U.S. states, mainly through interstate capital and credit markets.

We explore risk sharing patterns among European Community (EC) countries and among countries of the Organization for Economic Cooperation and Development (OECD) during 1966–90. A central finding is that about 40 percent of shocks to GDP are smoothed at the one-year frequency, with about half the smoothing achieved through national government budget deficits. At the three-year differencing frequency, only 20 percent of shocks to GDP are smoothed, with all the smoothing achieved through government lending and borrowing. An important implication is that the restrictions on budget deficits imposed by the 1992 Maastricht treaty may threaten the stability of the European economic and monetary union (EMU) in the absence of alternative risk sharing mechanisms. (Most EC countries are close to or above the maximum public-debt-to-GDP ratio allowed under Maastricht.)

Our methodology for measuring the amount of income and consumption smoothing achieved through various channels is based on a decomposition of the cross-country variance in GDP. Consider, for example, the national accounting identity GNP = GDP + net factor income. If there is smoothing through net factor income flows—namely, income smoothing via cross-country ownership of productive assets—GNP should have a smaller cross-sectional variance than GDP. Similarly, if there is consumption smoothing via saving, national consumption should have a smaller cross-sectional variance than national income. The cross-sectional variance decomposition of GDP enables us to measure the amount of cross-sectional smoothing achieved at each level of smoothing, as a fraction of shocks to GDP absorbed at that level.

Our results indicate that factor income flows do not smooth income across countries. This is true for the entire OECD group as well as for EC members, for the entire period as well as for two subperiods. Since factor income flows are an important component of income smoothing via capital markets, this suggests that European capital markets are less integrated than U.S. capital markets. We provide evidence in support of this interpretation.

We also find, for the period 1981–90, that the fraction of shocks to GDP smoothed via international transfers—including EC structural funds—is on the order of 3–6 percent, considerably less than the 13 percent fraction of shocks to the per capita gross state product smoothed by the federal government in the United States. The bulk of the income and consumption smoothing among OECD and EC countries is achieved through savings: countries save less in bad years. For the period 1966–90, we find that 40 percent of shocks to GDP of OECD countries are smoothed through this channel, with 60 percent of shocks not smoothed.

A back-of-the-envelope calculation reveals that if the EC wishes to achieve, through its budget, a degree of intercountry insurance comparable to that of the United States—namely, 25 percent of shocks to GDP not smoothed—the size of the budget has to increase dramatically, by some six to ten times. (The percentage of a shock to GDP not smoothed in the EC exceeds the percentage of a shock to gross state product not smoothed in the United States by about 35 percentage points. The fraction of a shock currently smoothed through the EC budget is 3–6 percent.) EMU may enhance capital market integration but this certainly cannot happen overnight. If monetary unification progresses according to schedule, the EC may have to provide greater inter-regional insurance until capital markets are sufficiently integrated to carry out this role, as they do in the United States.

Cross-country consumption smoothing can be achieved in several ways. Individuals in one country can save or dissave; the funds can then be transferred across country borders by financial intermediaries. Furthermore, the government of a country can borrow or lend internationally to smooth expenditure. Finally, corporations can choose to retain more or less profits; the retained profits can be invested in physical assets in the country where the corporation operates, or in financial assets; the funds may then finance investment in other countries. To get a sense of the relative importance for cross-country consumption smoothing of the various saving channels, we decompose total smoothing via saving to smoothing via personal, corporate, and government saving. We find that corporate and government saving are each responsible for about half the smoothing (about 20 percent of shocks to GDP smoothed by each component), and that there is no cross-country consumption smoothing through personal saving.

As noted above, the large amount of consumption smoothing achieved in the EC through government borrowing may not be sustainable in an EMU where fiscal coordination must be maintained. Until intercountry credit markets develop to allow substantial consumption smoothing through personal saving, the potential reduction in consumption smoothing via budget deficits of national governments may call for a yet greater insurance role for EC institutions, imposing a further burden on the EC budget.

Other researchers have looked into the cross-country smoothing role of net exports. Since saving is related to net exports through the identity $S = I + (X - M)$, the physical cross-country flows of goods generated by saving merits examination. We, therefore, decompose the smoothing through saving into smoothing via I and $X - M$, finding that all the smoothing is achieved through domestic net physical investment, with virtually no smoothing via net exports.

The finding that shocks to output are smoothed cross-sectionally through domestic net physical investment is consistent with the procyclical behavior of investment in aggregate U.S. data. The finding of zero cross-sectional smoothing via the current account is consistent with the well-known Feldstein-Horioka puzzle; that puzzle complements our finding that there is no smoothing through factor income flows and gives further indication of the limited cross-country risk sharing achieved via capital and credit markets among EC and OECD countries.

In our empirical analysis we deflate all the magnitudes (GDP, GNP, S, and so on) by the country consumption deflator. That is, we measure the national accounts figures of each country in terms of real consumption in that country. Of course, exchange rate fluctuations may affect consumption decisions and risk sharing patterns. If, for example, a country's currency appreciates in real (inflation adjusted) terms, the citizens and the government of that country can, in principle, purchase more goods at international prices with a given amount of the country's currency. We find, using our data, that this effect is very small, namely, that changes in the real exchange rate have a small effect on consumption patterns.

We do not examine the effects of labor mobility on smoothing of GDP shocks. Previous research has indicated that labor mobility among U.S. states smooths approximately 2.7 percent of an income shock at the annual frequency. Since labor mobility is lower among European countries and regions than among U.S. states, it is therefore unlikely that labor mobility among EC and OECD countries substantially affects risk-sharing patterns at the annual frequency.

Out in the Sunshine? Outsiders, Insiders, and The United States in 1998

Fabio Ghironi and Francesco Giavazzi

WE ADDRESS THE ISSUE OF THE OPTIMAL SIZE of the European currency union and intra-European Union exchange rate regime, focusing on the interactions among fiscal and monetary authorities in Europe, and between Europe and the rest of the world. Explicitly acknowledging the presence of the rest of the world—which, for simplicity, we call the United States—is essential to understanding the incentives and behavior of policy makers in and outside Europe.

Consider the institutional setup that, we believe, will most likely characterize the future operation of European economic and monetary union: frozen fiscal policies and noncooperative monetary policies under a European Monetary System (EMS)-2 regime in Europe. In this setup, our research supports the view that, so long as the size of the outsiders is non-negligible, central bankers would prefer the currency union to be relatively small, while the European Council of Economic and Finance Ministers (ECOFIN) would prefer it to be relatively large. The conflict arises because, in the absence of cooperation, the two face different trade-offs between output and inflation and therefore rank different outcomes differently. The only way to reach agreement between ECOFIN and the European central bank (ECB) on the size of the currency union is either by convincing the central banks of the ins and outs to cooperate (in which case the size of the currency union becomes irrelevant), or allowing governments to use fiscal policy actively in response to exogenous shocks. But the outsider central bank stands to loose from cooperating with the ECB—independent of the degree of fiscal policy activism and of the size of outsiders relative to insiders. Moreover, the outsider central bank always prefers to be left out of a relatively large currency union, because it can better exploit its ability to export inflation to the insiders by aggressively "riding" the more favorable output-inflation trade-off it faces. This suggests a potentially important reason (which, admittedly, may counter arguments favoring joining the single currency) why some states may be unwilling to join the currency union and, once they are out, their central banks may be unwilling to enter a cooperative agreement with the ECB.

Potential conflicts of interests can thus arise within one country over the optimal size of the currency union. Not only do we find a conflict between ECOFIN and the ECB under the EMS-2 regime in Europe, but also, while the outsider central bank always prefers being left out from a large currency union, the opposite holds for the outs' governments. Given a significant size for the outs, the latter would always prefer a small rather than a large currency union. This is because the larger the currency union, the more favorable the trade-off faced by the outs' central banks. Also the U.S. Federal Reserve and the U.S. government may disagree over the optimal size of the European currency union if an EMS-style regime were to be implemented in Europe, with the Fed preferring a small union and the U.S. government a large one. However, even if what happens in Europe affects welfare in the United States, it is unlikely that European policy makers will condition their choices about the size of the currency union on U.S. preferences.

Our paper suggests that in 1998, when the initial size of the currency union is decided, strategic interactions among players could result in considerable strain. This may be true irrespective of monetary and fiscal policy makers across countries having different preferences. The outcome will depend on the relative bargaining power of the various policy makers, as well as on other political considerations that our model does not capture—because the institutional framework within which policy makers interact will play a crucial role in the process.

Once the initial size of the currency union is determined, the natural evolution of the union itself, as dictated by the Maastricht treaty, will be in the direction of enlargement over time—eventually to cover the entire European Union. Such enlargement will require agreement on the part of the ins, but also of those previously out. Even if the potential conflicts between the ECB and the ECOFIN are resolved in favor of enlargement, the outs may not be attracted to joining the union.

Our analysis assumes that all players approach 1998 and the subsequent period starting from "equal initial conditions"—their economies being in equilibrium—and addresses the topic from the limited perspective of the optimal reactions to supply-side disturbances. Reality is far more complicated. In 1998, European countries are likely to be characterized by different economic situations. Outs may be outs either because they are not attracted to joining the union, or not accepted in it, or both. Most outsider economies may be classified as relatively weak, or plagued by significant disequilibria. If their governments do not have strong incentives to join the European currency union—and we suggest why this could happen—the process of enlargement envisioned in the Maastricht treaty could prove slower and more contentious than optimists believe.

Finally, another dimension of the choices that policy makers will face by 1998 merits attention: for a given initial size of the currency union, what will the optimal intra-European monetary arrangement be? We focus on the choice of the optimal size of the European currency union, but our results also provide tentative answers to the question of monetary arrangement. Consider, for example, the choice between a noncooperative EMS-2 regime and a noncooperative flexible exchange rate regime, absent the option to use fiscal policy to stabilize the economies.

When the European currency union includes all countries—except for a small open economy—all players are indifferent as to the exchange rate regime prevailing in Europe, which is intuitively justified by the absence of any impact of the outs' policy choices on the rest of the world. But when the outsiders are non-negligible, in most cases the EMS-2 regime turns out to be preferred to the flexible exchange rate regime. Controlling the exchange rate allows the outsiders' central bank to achieve a better outcome than would be achieved by controlling the money supply. Under the asymmetric regime, the employment loss is smaller and the outs' government is consequently better off. Therefore, at least if fixed fiscal policies and no cooperation represent a likely scenario, our findings suggest that the outs' authorities will favor an EMS-style regime over a flexible rate arrangement. Instead, we observe a conflict of interests between the ECB and the ECOFIN over what regime should be implemented. The ECB would like a flexible exchange rate regime to be adopted since this would allow it to achieve a significantly better inflation outcome by depriving the outs' central banks of control over the exchange rate. Nonetheless, this would come at the cost of higher employment losses, which lead the ECOFIN to prefer the managed exchange rate regime.

This further dimension of conflict among policy makers over the optimal features of the European currency union does not seem completely unlikely. As 1998 approaches, conflicts of interest among policy makers are likely to arise on the various issues. Dealing effectively with the conflicts will be necessary to ensure proper functioning of the European Union. Political developments and institutional design will undoubtedly play a crucial role.

Finally, our results show that the ability to use fiscal policy makes all authorities better off than if only monetary policy were used to react to supply-side shocks. This result may be interpreted as an argument against the rigid application of a fiscal stability pact in Europe. However, our modeling of fiscal policy is highly simplified. Indeed, if fiscal stability is interpreted as referring to the behavior of deficits and debts, active budget-balancing fiscal policies, as we consider in our paper, are not inconsistent with a fiscal stability pact.

Participants

Editors

Mario I. Blejer, Hebrew University and IMF
Leonardo Leiderman, Bank of Israel and Tel Aviv University
Assaf Razin, Tel Aviv University
David M. Cheney, IMF

Moderators

Mario I. Blejer, Hebrew University and IMF
June Flanders, Tel Aviv University
Charles E. Goodhart, London School of Economics
Leonardo Leiderman, Bank of Israel and Tel Aviv University
David Levhari, Hebrew University
Michael Michaely, Hebrew University
Assaf Razin, Tel Aviv University

Authors

Tamim Bayoumi, IMF
Roel M.W.J. Beetsma, Maastricht University
A. Lans Bovenberg, Netherlands Bureau for Economic Policy Analysis
Alex Cukierman, Tel Aviv University
Barry Eichengreen, University of California, Berkeley
Jacob A. Frenkel, Governor of the Bank of Israel
Fabio Ghironi, Universita Bocconi
Francesco Giavazzi, Universita Bocconi
Charles E. Goodhart, London School of Economics
Daniel Gros, CEPS
Manuel Guitián, IMF
Paul R. Masson, IMF

Robert A. Mundell, Columbia University
Richard Portes, London Business School and CEPR
Andrew K. Rose, Haas School of Business, University of California,
    Berkeley
Bent E. Sørenson, Brown University
Alfred Steinherr, European Investment Bank
William R. White, Bank for International Settlements
Oved Yosha, Tel Aviv University

Discussants

Benjamin Bental, Technion
Elise Brezis, Bar Ilan University
Zvi Eckstein, Tel Aviv University
Benjamin Eden, University of Haifa
Arye Hillman, Bar Ilan University
Ephraim Kleiman, Hebrew University
Nissan Leviatan, Hebrew University
Rafi Melnick, Bank of Israel
Enrique Mendoza, U.S. Federal Reserve Board
Nathan Sussman, Hebrew University
Alexander Swoboda, Graduate Institute of International Studies
Alfred Tovias, Hebrew University
Daniel Tsiddon, Tel Aviv University
Hirofumi Uzawa, Japan Development Bank

Other Participants

Carola Kaps, Frankfurter Allgemeine Zeitung
Martin Wolf, The Financial Times